Lionel Arthur Tollemache

Stones of Stumbling

Lionel Arthur Tollemache
Stones of Stumbling
ISBN/EAN: 9783743344143
Manufactured in Europe, USA, Canada, Australia, Japa
Cover: Foto ©ninafisch / pixelio.de

Manufactured and distributed by brebook publishing software (www.brebook.com)

Lionel Arthur Tollemache

Stones of Stumbling

WORKS

BY

THE HON. LIONEL A. TOLLEMACHE.

WITH SOME OPINIONS OF THE PRESS, ETC.

LONDON: WILLIAM RICE, 86 FLEET STREET, E.C.

[Sold also by BRENTANO, 17 Avenue de l'Opéra, Paris, and 31 Union Square, New York; TITTMANN, Dresden; VIEUSSEUX, Florence; PITHOEVER, Rome; and all Booksellers.]

ESSAYS, RECOLLECTIONS, AND CAUSERIES
By the Hon. LIONEL A. TOLLEMACHE.
[*Collected in their original form at MARK PATTISON'S request.*]

Demy 8vo, pp. 454, cloth, 5s.

SAFE STUDIES.

Contents:—

HISTORICAL PREDICTION. Sir G. C. LEWIS and LONGEVITY.
LITERARY EGOTISM. CHARLES AUSTIN.
RECOLLECTIONS of Mr. GROTE and Mr. BABBAGE.
Mr. TENNYSON'S SOCIAL PHILOSOPHY.
PHYSICAL and MORAL COURAGE. THE UPPER ENGADINE.
NOTES and RECOLLECTIONS of Sir CHARLES WHEATSTONE, DEAN STANLEY, and CANON KINGSLEY.
THE EPICURIST'S LAMENT. TRANSLATIONS.

POEMS and TRANSLATIONS.
BY
The Hon. Mrs. L. A. TOLLEMACHE.

Demy 8vo, pp. 238, cloth, 2s. 6d.

STONES OF STUMBLING.

Contents:—

THE CURE FOR INCURABLES. THE FEAR OF DEATH.
FEARLESS DEATHS. DIVINE ECONOMY OF TRUTH.

Appendices:—

RECOLLECTIONS of MARK PATTISON.* Mr. ROMANES'S CATECHISM.
NEOCHRISTIANITY and NEOCATHOLICISM: a Sequel.
* This is also published separately, demy 8vo, cloth, 1s.

☞ **These books are issued at COST PRICE.**

"The essays are mainly biographical, and are full of wit and humour. They abound in good stories of all kinds. Every page shows the classical humanist, the man of taste and scholarly refinement; but, like the essays of Montaigne, of whom Mr. Tollemache is almost an English counterpart, there is a richer vein of thought and of philosophy running through all this lighter matter."—*ANGLICAN CHURCH MAGAZINE.*

London: WILLIAM RICE, 86 Fleet Street, E.C.
(Sold also by Brentano, 17 Avenue de l'Opéra, Paris, and 31 Union Square, New York; Tittmann, Dresden; Vieusseux, Florence; Pithoever, Rome; and all Booksellers.)

"Mr. Tollemache's essays seem to us to possess literary merit of a rare and high order. He is not only pleasantly anecdotic; he is eminently sympathetic, ingenious, thoughtful, and appreciative, and many of these qualities are also exhibited in his more speculative and less personal papers. His recollections of Grote, Charles Austin, and Pattison are full of interesting anecdote and suggestive comment, while those of Babbage, Sir Charles Wheatstone, Dean Stanley, and Canon Kingsley, belong to the same order. We can best enforce our favourable judgment of these remarkable volumes by quoting a passage from a letter received from Pattison, to whom he had sent the privately printed edition, which of course did not contain the paper on Pattison himself:—' I should say that the papers on the whole show a union, which is very uncommon, of two opposite qualities—viz., a dominant interest in speculation of a wide and human character, with vast resources, in the memory, of single facts, incidents, or *mots* of famous men. How, with your eyesight, you ever compassed such a range of reading as is here brought to bear at all points of your argument must be a matter of wonder. It seems as if you could draw at pleasure upon all literature, from the classics down to Robert Montgomery and Swinburne.' In this judgment we cordially concur.—It should be added that the larger volume, entitled 'Safe Studies,' contains a series of graceful poems by Mrs. Tollemache. . . . The 'Recollections of Pattison' are very charming."—*THE TIMES.*

"These very interesting and, in part, very amusing volumes. . . . Altogether, we can give very hearty praise to the book, and that is something in the case of matter which has not the charm of novelty to the reviewer, and with a good deal of which he disagrees in opinion. Mr. Tollemache can tell an excellent story (such as that of the young lady who, having spoken enthusiastically about a clergyman, and being asked if she referred to any sermon of his, said, 'No; oh! no. But he hates *mayonnaise*, and so do I.'). He manages, though he himself is very frequently in presence, and the subject of discussion, never to be unpleasantly egotistic. His work has the literary flavour throughout, without being merely bookish, and he can argue a thesis like a craftsman and a master of his craft."—*SATURDAY REVIEW.*

"Mr. Tollemache is one of a fortunate few with whom a certain kind of memory may be said, as Rossetti said of beauty, to be a genius itself. . . . Even the anecdotes, good as they are, have scarcely the same literary value as his rare power of making men and women live before us with all their human charm and weakness, the charm the more real for the supplementary weakness, and the weakness itself winning our attachment in the light of the charm. His truly marvellous memory for details of speech and character may yet keep for us many a little trait, or passing word, which will hereafter be precious."—*SPEAKER.*

"The 'Safe Studies' are those to which it is impossible for any human creature to raise the smallest objection on any ground whatever, and they are about four times as long as the 'Stones of Stumbling.' These stumbling-blocks may possibly at some period or other have given scandal to a part of the population by no means likely to read them; but in these days the public has swallowed so many camels that we do not think Mr. Tollemache's gnats would even make any considerable portion of them cough. . . . We propose to make some observations on the most important of these charming essays. They are all singularly well worth reading, and may be described as the works of a most ingenious, accomplished, and cultivated man of leisure, who writes in order to fix recollections and systematize speculations which interest him, and not for the purpose of advocating particular views in the spirit of a partisan or propagandist. . . . The only likelihood of Charles Austin being remembered at all lies in the chance of the survival of the touching and striking account given of him by his accomplished, grateful, and most appreciative pupil."—The late Mr. Justice Fitzjames Stephen in *THE ST. JAMES'S GAZETTE.*

"He [the author] possesses in a high degree the first requisite of a biographer, the *admiratio Boswelliana*, and he combines with the exact memory of Mr. Hayward some of the sympathetic appreciativeness of Lord Houghton. . . . This ('Stones of Stumbling') includes the 'Recollections of [Mark] Pattison,' which attracted so much attention on their first appearance in the *Journal of Education.* Together with the notice of Charles Austin (in 'Safe Studies'), it must also possess a permanent value, as an unrivalled example of Boswellian portraiture—with the added interest that, in recording the traits of his friends, the author is half-unconsciously revealing some of his own."—*ACADEMY.*

"Since the death of Hayward, we know no English *littérateur* who has, in the same degree as Mr. Tollemache, the happy knack of recollecting or collecting the characteristic sayings and doings of a distinguished man, and piecing them together in a finished mosaic."
—*DAILY CHRONICLE.*

LONDON: WILLIAM RICE, 86 FLEET STREET, E.C.

[Sold also by BRENTANO, 17 Avenue de l'Opéra, Paris, and 31 Union Square, New York; TITTMAN, Dresden; VIEUSSEUX, Florence; PITHOEVER, Rome; and all Booksellers.

"Mr. Tollemache has at last overcome his dislike to publicity, and has given the world at large a series of delightful studies which might otherwise have been well-nigh lost in the sombre and dissipated retirement of a bound periodical. . . . An atmosphere of soft melancholy envelops his treatment; and this melancholy is perhaps the cause of yet another charm. His studies are not only full of 'unfamiliar quotations from familiar authors,' but abound in pleasant and witty digressions."—*NATIONAL OBSERVER.*

"The Hon. Lionel Tollemache abounds in witty sentences, and excels in the art of stringing together good things."—*WHITEHALL REVIEW.*

"The books, as a whole, give in an agreeable form an outline or suggestion of all that has been most prominent and characteristic for the past twenty or thirty years in the leading currents of speculative thought in England. Though they deal with thorny problems, and sometimes argue closely enough to be hard reading, the essays have the charm which the judicious use of a wide learning gives, and the book is attractive as well as thoughtful and suggestive."—*SCOTSMAN.*

"That Mr. Tollemache has an inexhaustible fund of anecdotes is not saying much; but what is remarkable is the skill, the aptness, the felicity with which he applies them. . . . Mrs. Tollemache's poems are penetrated with a love of nature truly Wordsworthian. . . . It has been long since we read anything so interesting, amusing, and delightful as 'Safe Studies.'"—*GALIGNANI'S MESSENGER.*

"The essays include 'Mr. Tennyson's Social Philosophy,' 'Charles Austin,' 'Physical and Moral Courage,' 'Recollections of Dean Stanley,' and other papers, making one of the most interesting of books. Even more interesting, if possible, are the 'Recollections of [Mark] Pattison,' which form part of the companion volume. . . . There are enough good stories in Mr. Tollemache's Recollections to fill half-a-dozen columns."—*STAR.*

"Both these volumes have been previously printed for private circulation, and in this form have found their way to the British Museum and other great libraries. They have now been reprinted and published 'at cost price,' and may almost be said to mark an epoch in the history of cheap books. . . . In all these essays Mr. Tollemache shows himself to be a worthy follower of Boswell, and is content for the most part to allow his characters to reveal themselves by the anecdotes and fragments of conversation which he is able to report. These are mostly

London : WILLIAM RICE, 86 Fleet Street, E.C.

[Sold also by Brentano, 17 Avenue de l'Opéra, Paris, and 31 Union Square, New York; Tittmann, Dresden; Vieusseux, Florence; Pithoever, Rome; and all Booksellers.]

well told and to the point, and make the essays very pleasant reading."
—*GUARDIAN.*

"The studies are intensely interesting, as all know who have at all followed the movement of thought in the last twenty or twenty-five years. ["Stones of Stumbling"] A dainty dish relished by intellectual epicures."—*ANTI-JACOBIN.*

"Many years ago the Hon. Lionel Tollemache printed two volumes of essays, entitled 'Safe Studies' and 'Stones of Stumbling,' which he gave away to his friends. When it was known that these volumes contained pleasant recollections of Mark Pattison, Dean Stanley, George Grote, and other well-known men, to say nothing of singularly felicitous criticisms upon Tennyson, &c., it was natural that even those who were not personal friends should inquire about the books, and to each and all of the inquirers, I believe, Mr. Tollemache presented the pair of handsome volumes. The result was that almost every newspaper reviewed the books, although they boasted no publisher and were not on sale in the bookshops. Now, therefore, when the time seems to have come for publication, Mr. William Rice, of Fleet Street, who has the task in hand, is able to lead off with quite a chorus of acclamations from the daily and weekly press, beginning with the *Times*, which refers to the 'literary merit of a rare and high order' which is to be found in these essays, and ending with the New York *Nation*, which tells us that the 'Recollections of Pattison' are 'thoroughly delightful' —as indeed they are. Mark Pattison has received rather brutal treatment lately at the hands of Mr. Swinburne; but it is pleasant to turn to him here as a scholar in an age of superficiality, as a genuinely learned bookman at a time when so many of us are merely veritable butterflies, sipping a smattering of knowledge from every passing volume. Then Mr. Tollemache's anecdotes are so good. One can never forget the dying Pattison asking for some of his favourite volumes, stroking them lovingly, and pondering whether he will have his books in heaven. And then there is the story of the young lady who, having spoken enthusiastically of a certain clergyman, and being asked if she referred to any sermon of his, said: 'No; oh, no. But he hates *mayonnaise*, and so do I.' Truly these are delightful tomes."—*THE QUEEN.*

"Two admirable volumes... Mr. Tollemache is a most accomplished and attractive writer. He is a man of philosophic insight and

---

LONDON: WILLIAM RICE, 86 FLEET STREET, E.C.

[Sold also by BRENTANO, 17 Avenue de l'Opéra, Paris, and 31 Union Square, New York; TITTMANN, Dresden; VIEUSSEUX, Florence; PITHOEVER, Rome; and all Booksellers.]

culture, his information is large and various, and his imaginative and humorous powers are considerable, and are frequently displayed with effect. . . . It is a misfortune for English literature in its higher and more serious departments that bad health should have prevented Mr. Tollemache from contributing to it with greater constancy and copiousness than he has been able to do. The opinion which was evidently entertained of him by many men of extraordinary mental power and consummate learning would then undoubtedly have been more generally shared."—*THE WORLD.*

"["Mr. Tennyson's Social Philosophy"] in an admirable volume of Essays I have just read, 'Safe Studies.'"—*TRUTH.*

"It is well that they should be put in the way of a wide circulation, for they contain much of unquestionable interest and value. . . . Mr. Tollemache's range of subject is tolerably large. His method of treatment is agreeably individual—honest, frank, and direct to the point."—*THE GLOBE.*

"We know of no book in the English language more interesting when considered from the point of view from which it is written. As a story-teller Mr. Tollemache is unrivalled, and his knowledge of men and things is almost marvellous. He has also the happy knack of gathering into a beautiful mosaic the sayings and doings of distinguished men."—*THE CHRISTIAN COMMONWEALTH.*

"One of the most delightful papers in these fruity books is that on Mark Pattison, but all of the writing impresses one as the overheard talk of a delightful conversationalist, whose memory is stored with riches, and who knows the best society in men and books."—*ATLANTIC MONTHLY.*

"The volumes are witty and interesting, and besprinkled throughout with the dew of wide and unusual reading. Particularly in his resort to apt classical quotation does Mr. Tollemache preserve an honourable literary tradition in a way which now seems a little old-fashioned, though agreeable from its very quaintness as well as its frequent pungency. . . . The 'Recollections of Pattison' are thoroughly delightful. Based upon a long friendship, and upon a certain affinity, they are altogether charming in their mingled analysis and reminiscence, narrative and anecdote. . . . We take pleasure in commending these books for their biographical interest, which in parts is of the greatest, as well as for the refinement and learning that pervade them throughout."—*THE NATION (New York).*

LONDON : WILLIAM RICE, 86, FLEET STREET, E.C.

[Sold also by BRENTANO, 17 Avenue de l'Opéra, Paris, and 31 Union Square, New York; TITTMAN, Dresden; VIEUSSEUX, Florence; PITHOEVER, Rome; and all Booksellers.]

"These books contain biographical papers that, in form and importance, rank with the best work of their class in the English language. The author has the rare gift of being able to paint portraits instead of making photographs, and he has cultivated this now almost lost art until it has reached perfection. . . . The vein of deep philosophy that runs through these essays is made most attractive by the wit that sparkles in every line."—*BOOK CHAT* (*New York*).

"The special quality in these essays which makes them worthy of preservation and continuance is the quality which Mr. Matthew Arnold used to call 'sweet reasonableness.' Here is an Englishman without insularity, a writer on theological topics without prejudices, a gentleman without undue exclusiveness, a classicist without over-punctiliousness. . . . The most abiding impression that one receives from the reading of all these delightful personal sketches is that of the personality of the author himself. He has made his characters live before us, and his own figure is among them—long to be remembered."—*THE OUTLOOK*, or *CHRISTIAN UNION* (*New York*).

"I find your article [*Fortnightly Review*, July, 1892] charming, and your Whiggism mild. Neither epithet is, I think, exaggerated."—*Letter from Mr. GLADSTONE*.

LONDON : WILLIAM RICE, 86 FLEET STREET, E.C.
Sold also by BRENTANO, 17 Avenue de l'Opéra, Paris, and 31 Union Square, New York ; TITTMANN, Dresden ; VIEUSSEUX, Florence ; PITHOEVER, Rome ; and all Booksellers.]

STONES OF STUMBLING.

STONES OF STUMBLING.

BY THE

Hon. LIONEL A. TOLLEMACHE.

"Jérusalem est sortie plus brillante et plus belle du travail en apparence destructeur de la science moderne. Les pieux récits dont on berça notre enfance sont devenus, grâce à une saine interprétation, de hautes vérités; et c'est à nous qui voyons Israël dans sa réelle beauté, c'est à nous autres critiques qu'il appartient vraiment de dire: *Stantes erant pedes nostri in atriis tuis, Jerusalem.*"—RENAN.

FOURTH EDITION,

WITH TWO APPENDICES.

LONDON:
WILLIAM RICE, 86 FLEET STREET, E.C.

1895.

AC
8
T55
1895

PREFACE

TO THE FIRST PUBLISHED EDITION.

Σμικρὸς ἐξαρκεῖ λόγος.—SOPHOCLES.
("A short account suffices.")

In the *Preface to the Published Edition of "Safe Studies,"* I have alluded to the conditions under which my two volumes, after a long process of incubation, or rather of domestic rearing, have been suddenly left to make shift for themselves. Readers of this volume are referred to that Preface, which contains some needful explanations, and is, in fact, an *Apologia pro scriptis meis*.

LIONEL A. TOLLEMACHE.

ATHENÆUM CLUB,
   PALL MALL, S.W.
   1891.

PREFACE

TO THE SECOND PUBLISHED EDITION.

"In poetry, a certain faith in the impossible, and in religion, a also faith in the unknowable, must have a place."—GOETHE.

In the *Preface to the First Published Edition* of this volume, it is stated that the *Preface to Safe Studies* " contains some needful explanations, and is, in fact, an *Apologia pro scriptis meis*." As, however, I find that many persons who have read *Stones of Stumbling* have not seen *Safe Studies*, or at least have not sought out the "needful explanations," I subjoin, with a few corrections and additions, the passage in *Safe Studies* to which I chiefly refer:—

"The last time that Mr. Matthew Arnold wrote to me was after his perusal of my *Mr. Romanes's Catechism*. His letter contains these words: 'I consider myself, to adopt your very good expression, a Liberal Anglican; and I think the times are in favour of our being allowed so to call ourselves.' On the other hand, Mr. Hamerton, in his *French and English*, has expressed some friendly surprise at my calling myself an Anglican of any sort. His surprise will doubtless be shared by many readers of *Stones of Stumbling*. Let me, therefore, explain that my *Divine Economy of Truth* was written before the reaction from my Evangelical education had subsided, and before the Anglican Gospel had suddenly and, as it were, unwittingly changed from tidings of unspeakable sadness to tidings of unspeakable joy, inasmuch as that ghastly nightmare, the belief in unending torments, then weighed on the English Church, as it still weighs on the Roman Church. The result is that this Essay contains several expressions which I should not use now, and is marked by a combativeness and even a bitterness which are, I hope, laid aside in my somewhat similar Essay written ten years later under the title of *Neochristianity and Neocatholicism*. It should, however, be noted that the main contention of those articles has now been practically admitted by Canon Cheyne in his *Bampton Lectures*, by the Principal of Pusey House in *Lux Mundi*, and, more recently, by those official representatives of orthodox learning in our two Universities, Canon Driver and Canon Kirkpatrick.

"To me certainly it seems that one who accepts and assimilates the results of criticism is more and more disposed to give a response to the grand utterances of the Hebrew Scriptures—to that amazing confidence which has been so abundantly justified, and to those more amazing prophecies which have been almost literally fulfilled. Thus we are in a manner led to share the confidence shown in such texts as: '*O pray for the peace of Jerusalem; they shall prosper that love thee. The Lord hath chosen Zion to be an habitation for himself; he hath longed for her.*' And we can, at least, put our own construction—perhaps a wider and deeper one than was originally intended—on the prophecies: '*The Gentiles shall come to thy light, and kings to the brightness of thy rising. In those days it shall come to pass that ten men shall take hold out of all languages of the nations, even shall take hold of the skirt of him that is a Jew, saying: We will go with you, for we have heard that God is with you.*'"

If I were now to rewrite my article on the *Divine Economy of Truth*, I should leave its main scope and argument as they stand, but should profoundly modify its tone, and, in particular, I should omit certain passages which may have had their use when Neochristianity was still militant, or rather when it was regarded as a sort of rebel with no claim to belligerent rights, but which would now be wholly superfluous; and, having made these alterations, I should be disposed to call the volume, not *Stones of Stumbling*, but *Bulwarks of Belief*.

Charles Austin was fond of quoting the passage in *Absalom and Achitophel* in which Dryden adverts to the change wrought by the Reformation in the relative position of Catholics and Protestants, whom he respectively designates as Jebusites and Israelites:

"The inhabitants of old Jerusalem
Were Jebusites; the town so called from them;
And theirs the ancient right.
But, when the chosen people grew more strong,
The rightful cause at length became the wrong."

May not the new and greater Reformation have now proceeded so far that the wrongful cause, as it was but lately thought, is fast becoming the right one? In illustration of the gradual but complete change that has been coming over men's minds during the last two centuries, I will quote Mark Pattison's comment on the theology of *Paradise Lost*: "It would have been a thing incredible to Milton that the hold of the Jewish Scriptures over the imagination of English men and women could ever be weakened. This process, however, has already commenced. The demonology of the poem has already, with educated readers, passed from the region of fact into that of fiction. Not so universally, but with a large number of readers, the angelology can be no more than what the critics call machinery."

Well might Sophocles exclaim:

ἅπανθ' ὁ μακρὸς κἀναρίθμητος χρόνος
φύει τ' ἄδηλα καὶ φανέντα κρύπτεται.

"Vast and measureless time brings to light all that is hidden, and hides all that has been brought to light."

But, if haply we are oppressed with the sense of the universal flux of things spiritual as of things physical—with something of Tennyson's foreboding that our religious systems "have their day and cease to be"—let us fortify ourselves by recalling Matthew Arnold's paraphrase of Monica's last prayer, his rendering of that prayer into its modern equivalent:

> "Creeds pass, rites change, no altar standeth whole.
> Yet we her memory, as she prayed, will keep,
> Keep by this: *Life in God, and union there.*"

LIONEL A. TOLLEMACHE.

March, 1893.

NOTE TO FOURTH EDITION.

As non-classical readers have often complained of being baffled by my classical quotations, I have thought it better in bringing out a new edition of my volumes to subjoin an Index, with translations, of those quotations.

L. A. T.

PREFACE
TO FIRST EDITION.

Τελείων ἐστιν ἡ στερεὰ τροφή.—Heb. v. 14.

ALL these articles are reprinted from the *Fortnightly Review*. It is with some hesitation that I include in the volume the plea which, eleven years ago (*calidâ juventâ*), I set up on behalf of Euthanasia. In the additions which are now made to the article, and especially in the *Note* at the end of it, I endeavour to explain that I am merely expounding and defending against logical objections Sir Thomas More's summary proposal for the Relief of Incurables in Utopia. He assuredly sought not to naturalize his scheme among the subjects of Henry VIII.; and I, too, am in nowise ambitious of introducing it among the subjects of Queen Victoria! The reform, if ever it is to be,

"lies so far away,
Not in our time, nor in our children's time,—
'Tis like the second world to us that live."

Let it therefore be understood, once for all, that

my article is *philosophical discussion*—it is not a revolutionary propaganda.

The article on *Physical Courage* in my other series, and those on *The Fear of Death* and *Fearless Deaths* in this one, together made up in their original form the single article on *Courage and Death* (Jan. 1876); they are, however, reprinted with considerable additions.

L. A. T.

1884.

The Second Edition is a reprint of the First, with the *Recollections of Pattison* added as an Appendix.

1885.

Mr. Romanes's Catechism and *Neochristianity and Neocatholicism* have been added more recently.

1887.

CONTENTS.

	PAGE
THE CURE FOR INCURABLES	1
THE FEAR OF DEATH	32
FEARLESS DEATHS...	51
DIVINE ECONOMY OF TRUTH	66

APPENDIX I.

RECOLLECTIONS OF PATTISON 119

APPENDIX II.

MR. ROMANES'S CATECHISM	207
NEOCHRISTIANITY AND NEOCATHOLICISM: A SEQUEL ...	228

TRANSLATIONS OF GREEK, LATIN, AND GERMAN QUOTATIONS IN THE TEXT 238

STONES OF STUMBLING.

THE CURE FOR INCURABLES.*

κρεῖσσον γὰρ εἰσάπαξ θανεῖν
ἢ τὰς ἁπάσας ἡμέρας πάσχειν κακῶς.

ÆSCHYLUS.

ALL persons who feel a lively interest in the mitigation of human suffering, should rejoice that the very interesting essay on *Euthanasia*,† which originally appeared among the *Birmingham Essays*, has been published in a separate form. Even those who do not altogether agree with Mr. Williams, should at least wish that the plan he suggests should be brought under discussion. His proposal is, that in cases of incurable and painful illness the doctors should be allowed, with the patient's consent, and after taking all neces-

* *Fortnightly Review*, Feb. 1873.
† *Euthanasia.* By S. D. Williams, jun.; with preface by Rose Mary Crawshay. Williams & Norgate. 1872. Third edition.

sary safeguards, to administer so strong an anæsthetic as to render all future anæsthetics superfluous; in short, that there should be a sort of legalized suicide by proxy. The advantages that would follow such a system are so obvious, that it is unnecessary to read the horrible instance given by Mrs. Crawshay in her preface, to be reminded of them. ✗Any of us may one day have to bear—many of us will certainly have to witness —either cancer, creeping paralysis, or something equally unpleasant; some may even have to endure the hardest fate of all—the fate of a mortally-wounded soldier, who wishes to die, but whose wounds are laboriously tended; so that, by an ingenious cruelty, he is kept suffering, against nature, and against his own will.* Hence, even from the most selfish point of view, we all have an interest that this question should be speedily discussed; so that, in case any change should be thought possible

* It is probably from surgical cases that the strongest arguments for Euthanasia may be drawn. One of the highest authorities respecting such cases, Sir Benjamin Brodie, said that a very moderate amount of pain, if continued for a long time, would make one heartily tired of life. He remarked also, that during his whole life he had known only two dying persons who showed any fear of death; and that both those died of bleeding. One cause of this singular circumstance probably was, that in these two cases there was hardly any pain to distract the mind; and the fact is curious as showing how rare, in Sir Benjamin's experience, such painless deaths must have been.

and right, some foreshadowing of that change may appear in our lifetime.*

Still, though one fully acknowledges the ability of the essay, there are certain portions of it to which one may give only a partial assent. There will, however, probably be some readers of these pages who have not seen the original pamphlet; while with the popular arguments on the other side all are sure to be familiar. And it may therefore be advisable that I should, so to say, *hold a brief on behalf of Euthanasia*,† and state Mr. Williams's case as strongly as I can, including one or two points to which, I may venture to think, he has not paid sufficient attention.

The evils arising from the present method, or want of method, are forcibly stated by Mr. Williams. It is needless for me to repeat his painfully graphic account of what I cannot but hope is an exceptional death-bed scene, of the

* See *Note* at the end of the article.

† [I call attention to these words, because some of my critics are mistaken as to the manner and degree in which I uphold Euthanasia (see the *Preface* to this volume). In dealing with so unfamiliar a topic, it was above all things needful to be plain and incisive; and I was therefore glad when the *Spectator* described the style of the article as "defiantly clear." Had I been stating my views judicially instead of holding a brief, some of my general propositions would have been qualified. My language would then have been less defiant; but would it have been as clear? (1883.)

agony which grows daily worse and worse, and which may "possibly culminate in almost unimaginable horror." If a summary remedy could be applied to this suffering, there would be the further advantage that persons of a morbid and brooding nature might gain confidence through life, and that, knowing that death would be deprived of its sting, they would have a sort of negative stimulus, or (if I may so say) an anti-preventive to exertion. Then, again, we must consider the friends who, besides the immediate suffering of nursing the sick man, often permanently impair their constitutions and nervous systems, and who, moreover, are thus exposed to a sort of moral suicide; I mean, they curtail their own powers of usefulness far more than a dose of laudanum would curtail those of their dying friend. It should also be observed that if, on these accounts, the legalizing of a modified *Hari-kuri* in England be reckoned a good, the good would in each case be much increased by the force of example; each person who availed himself of the new method of giving relief to himself and his friends, would be doing what in him lay to break down the old prejudice, and to make the proceedings, so to say, fashionable, and would thus be a public as well as a private benefactor. On the whole, it cannot be doubted that the benefits resulting from a change in the law would be simply enormous; so that, unless a yet more enormous advantage can be shown to follow from obliging the sufferers to die in agony, the Euthanasiasts must be admitted to have gained the day. The *onus probandi* clearly rests with the opponents of the scheme. Those opponents may be roughly divided into two classes—the theological or sentimental opponents, and the more rational opponents. It is with the former class (whose objections, after all, possibly lie at the root of the other objections) that Mr. Williams deals almost exclusively; and to these his answer is overwhelming.

It is urged that Providence ordains the day of our death, and that to hasten that day is an act of rebellion against the Divine will. In truth, however, as God is a good being, his will must be to promote the happiness of his creatures; and, therefore, to say that Euthanasia, though tending to human happiness, is against the Divine will, is like saying that it both does tend to happiness and does not. But the fact is, that, when people thus speak of the Divine will, they conceive it to be embodied and represented in the order of nature; just as, in like manner, a line of conduct, otherwise expedient, is so constantly objected to as not being *natural*. The truth, however, is that, since many portentous evils exist in nature, whenever we remedy those evils, we, as it were, mend nature. It is natural and, on the hypothesis, in obedience to the Divine ordinance, that when we walk in the rain, we should get wet; and yet we do that most unnatural and impious thing —we hold up umbrellas. As Mr. Williams epigrammatically puts it, "Man's whole existence, so far as it is not blindly passive, ... consists, if the phrase quoted have any real meaning, in systematic opposition to the will of God." Indeed, St. Paul's celebrated defence of passive obedience might be almost literally paraphrased thus :—" Things which be, are ordained of God ; whoso, therefore, alters things which be, alters the ordinance of God; and they that alter shall receive to themselves damnation." It is from this theological optimism that the opposition spoken of by Comte has arisen between the theological and the industrial spirit ;* and it is

* Nequicquam deus abscidit
Prudens Oceano dissociabili
   Terras, si tamen impiæ
Non tangenda rates transilimnt vada.

Herodotus mentions a Greek colony living on an isthmus, who wished to protect themselves against the Persians by turning their isthmus into an island; but the oracle forbad them, " for Zeus would have made it an island if he wished." In a similar spirit, watches, according to Mr. Baden Powell, were at first denounced as unchristian, for telling the time more enough for our present purpose to say that the arguments which would forbid the prevention of the suffering incident to death, would forbid the prevention of any suffering whatever. But, it is said, the pain of death ought to be endured, as we are told in the Bible that death is the penalty of sin. I reply, in the first place, that this argument, if worth anything, would forbid, not merely the extinction of such pain, but its partial mitigation (as by opiates). Also, as Mr. Williams argues, all suffering is represented as the effect of sin, and especially the suffering of childbirth. And the Evangelicals were quite consistent in the opposition that they raised to the use of chloroform in confinements, until, fortunately, public opinion became too strong for them. May not their own logic be turned against them, if it should one day appear that the uses of the sedative in childbirth and before death involve the same principle, and must stand and fall together?

Allied to these objections is the sentimental remark that suicide is cowardly. Mr. Williams answers that a man of sound mind, who has nerve to destroy himself, whatever he may be, is certainly not a coward. But I would chiefly lay

accurately than the sun. It is well-known that some early Christians objected to shaving, as defacing the image of God. What do orthodox shavers make of this objection?

stress on the fact that here again there is no difference in kind between the suffering of a lingering death and other suffering. If it is cowardly to avoid the former, it is equally cowardly to avoid the latter. So that, according to these reasons, the mother who has taken chloroform is a double coward : * she has shirked the divinely appointed pain, and has not braved the " ills that she knows not of."

Much is also said about the sacredness of life—just as men used to talk about the divine right of kings. It is now generally admitted that the authority of kings is divine only in the sense in which all authority is divine; and, as the essayist truly says, "it may well be doubted if life have any sacredness about it, apart from the use to be made of it by its possessor." Indeed, life is the mere framework or shell of what Juvenal calls the *vivendi causas.* Yet all the high ends of life—all our means of general usefulness—we are willing to sacrifice for some special mode of bettering the condition of our species. And he who would devote all that makes life worth having to the

* Unless, as has been often asserted, there is almost always a slight risk in giving chloroform (so recently as during the late war, both French and German surgeons were said to be very chary in giving it). If the risk is increased by chloroform in ever so slight a degree, whoever incurs the increased risk is morally guilty of euthanasia.

common good (including his own), and yet has scruples about sacrificing for the same object a few days of agonized existence, is like a man who lavishes his grain, but treasures up the worthless husks.

But this is not all. Among the talents which men thus devote to the public good are included health and strength; and these, it need hardly be said, are potentialities of life. Statistics seem to show that the best chance of reaching old age is by living, as it were, in cotton-wool, and by exerting one's brain only just so much as may be necessary either to earn one's bread, or to keep the mind from preying on itself. Every one who does more than this diminishes the value of his life, and is what I may call a slow suicide. Indeed, it would be easy to make a goodly series of classes and conditions of men, from sportsmen to martyrs, who have acted in a way which would be regarded by any insurer as opposed to long life, and who, therefore,—if the hackneyed, but most inexact phrase has any meaning,—have taken measures "to quit their post without awaiting their commander's bidding." Of course, it may be said that the martyrs, when they die, are obeying a Divine summons, as they have hastened their end from noble motives; but it may fairly be asked whether we have a right to censure the motives of a man who declines to prolong wantonly the suffering of himself and his family; in other words, who provideth for his own, and also for those of his own house.

Nor is it only in dealing with their individual selves that men are disposed to neglect the sacredness of life. They certainly are not more scrupulous about the lives of their neighbours. "Hitherto," as the essayist observes, "man has shown as little sense of the value of man's life as Nature herself, whenever his passions, or lusts, or interests have been thwarted by his brother man, or have seemed likely to be forwarded by his brother man's destruction."

There are, moreover, other instances more closely resembling Euthanasia,[*] in which the medical attendant of a dying man, from however kindly motives, seems to touch the sacred thing, and should beware of the fate of Uzzah. Mr. Williams supposes an ingeniously extreme case of the sort, which shall be given in his own words:—

"Suppose, for instance, that a given patient were certain to drag on through a whole month of hideous suffering, if left to himself and nature, but that the intensity of his sufferings could be allayed by drugs, which, nevertheless, would hasten the known inevitable end by a week;—there are few, if any,

---

[*] Here, as elsewhere, I use this term with special reference to the case of incurables, and I so distinguish it from the more general term, Suicide.

medical men who would hesitate to give the drugs; few, if any, patients, or patients' relations or friends, who would hesitate to ask that they should be given. And if this be so, what becomes of the sacredness of life? . . . . Is it not clear that, if you once break in upon life's sacredness, if you curtail its duration by never so little, the same reasoning that justifies a minute's shortening of it, will justify an hour's, a day's, a week's, a month's, a year's; and that all subsequent appeal to the inviolability of life is vain?"

I can, from my own knowledge, give an instance not unlike this. Not many years ago, in one of the eastern counties, a country gentleman died, who had long been almost hopelessly ill. As soon as his case was given up, his doctors gave him a sedative, which they refused to give him before, and which much relieved his suffering. Now, so striking are the recoveries of persons whose cases have been despaired of, that the saying, "While there is life there is hope," has passed into a proverb; and, just as Hallam speaks of that extreme form of expediency which we call necessity, so in medical matters it is an inappreciable amount of hope which is really denoted by the word "hopeless." And, therefore, when in the present case the sedative, which had before been refused as likely to extinguish all chance of recovery, was at last given, a course was adopted which made the assurance of death doubly sure. In confirmation of instances such as the foregoing, it may be added, that I am told on medical authority that in the last stages of cancer, and still more in hopeless cases of burning and of contusions of the lower parts of the body, it is now not uncommon to give strong narcotics, which, while they much mitigate the final agony, by no means tend to prolong it.*

I have now endeavoured to dispose of the chief theological objections to the principle of euthanasia; but two such objections remain, which relate to matters of detail; and I glance at these arguments, not from any sense of their intrinsic merits, but because the prejudice on this subject is so inveterate, that the air must be well cleared of its influence before the various aspects of suicide can be properly discussed. One of the objections was raised in a quarter which, I own, a little surprised me:—

"Imagine the horror of the situation, if by some accident —and such an accident would not surely be impossible—the sufferer should not lose consciousness at once, and finding

---

* More than one Englishman when, travelling in hot or plague-stricken countries, where burial follows as soon as possible after death, has been known to beg, that in case anything should happen to him, his friends would apply a "bare bodkin" to his body before his interment. Need I add that any one who has entertained such a wish has committed euthanasia already in his heart? What business has he to rob himself of the few moments of smothering in his coffin, which a merciful Providence might vouchsafe to him for repentance, and to rush, with suicide in his right hand, into the presence of his offended Maker?

his courage fail, as the courage of suicides often does fail, at the felt approach of death, were vainly to beg for the life which it would be then impossible to restore!"*

I apprehend that after any decisive step in one's life—marriage, for example—it is a very sad thing if one repents when it is too late. But a wise man will first determine what seems to him best, and then will not much trouble himself about the possibility of future repentance—certainly not of a repentance which may be caused by the nervous prostration of disease. Also, between marriage and euthanasia there is this difference: the husband of a scold may have to bemoan his lot through many long years; while, in the other case, if chloroform is the remedy chosen, the time available for inopportune regrets is somewhat limited. The other objection is mentioned, or forestalled, by Mr. Williams. Some persons, according to him, object, or will object, to his scheme because it would deprive us of the purifying influence of ministering at a bed of sickness; and his answer is, in effect, that there will still be sick beds at which to minister. An opponent might, however, suggest that, if the new system were carried out to its possible consequences, some of us, at any rate, might lose this hallowing privilege. I should, therefore, prefer

* *Spectator*, March 18th, 1871.

giving the more general answer that this objection, like so many of the preceding ones, would apply, not to mortal sickness only, but to all suffering. If pain is sent by God's ordinance as a schooling either to its victims or to its witnesses, is it not blasphemous presumption ever to try to relieve it? Much danger, according to this theory, is to be apprehended from the everlasting painlessness of heaven. And, even on earth, might it not be prudent in the Government to torture for our benefit a few clergymen at stated intervals, that they may not merely excite our sympathy by their sufferings, but also set us an example of Christian resignation?

To sum up this part of the case. Either we are bound, in all possible ways, to stretch to the utmost the elastic thread of life, or we are not. If we are so bound, nearly all of us are guilty of great wickedness. But, if there are any limits to this duty, human reason must be the judge of those limits, and human welfare must be their test. In other words, the question of euthanasia should not be theologically prejudged, but should be discussed on purely social grounds. In case this important point should not even yet be clear to all readers, I will try to illustrate it yet further as I go on.

One of the most interesting parts of Mr. Lecky's

work on *European Morals*,* is that in which he exhibits the contrast between the extreme indifference to suicide which prevailed in the first century of our era, and the utter abhorrence of it which was introduced by the Christian Church. Possibly, in this matter, modern Liberalism is tending, as Aristotle would have said, to a mean, but inclines towards the former of the two extremes. Some one has said that the course of history, though it does not go in circles, goes in a sort of spiral; and it may be that in regard to suicide, as in regard to sundry other points, we are now coming to a curve which brings us nearer to the ancient point of view, than to the point of view of modern Catholicism. The Catholic point of view is briefly this: that suicide, essentially, is as sinful as ordinary murder; while, accidentally, it has the further little drawback that since, unless the act is clumsily done, it leaves scarce a moment for repentance, it almost certainly involves everlasting perdition.† This Catholic dogma is

---

* Mr. Lecky speaks approvingly of a saying of Bacon's, to the effect that physicians should regard euthanasia (the word, of course, being used in an extended sense) as the great end of their art. To attain this desirable object, do we require new anæsthetics, or merely a more thorough application of those now in use?

† The true Christian spirit is surely not opposed to euthanasia. If that spirit is expressed in the Golden Rule, and exemplified in the conduct of the good Samaritan, it

clearly connected with the excessive importance which many have attached to a man's state of mind on his death-bed, and which has found expression in the sacrament of "extreme unction." But with so horrible a superstition, and even with the prayer against sudden death which is contained in our own Litany, few thoughtful persons now really sympathize. There are also other signs that the popular opinion about suicide is undergoing a rapid change. One of the most curious of those signs is, that a writer so little addicted to new ideas as Archbishop Whately should have said that suicide is merely an exaggerated form of wasting time, in so far as it is a kind of idleness which cannot be made up for by extra work afterwards. But, on the other hand, a suicide is far less culpable than a prolonged idler: the suicide's fault is, at worst, a negative one; while the idler is a living burden on society; for he is an unproductive consumer, or, as a distinguished writer expresses it, a do-nothing-eat-all. With this reservation, then, Whately's *dictum* may be taken as fairly expressing the opinion of the wisest of the ancients concerning suicide, namely, that the man is to blame who wantonly deprives

enjoins us to relieve suffering, and not to leave it alone. Nor can the promise of heaven fail to offer to the dying Christian an inducement to use all lawful means to hasten his entrance thither.

his country of his services. But it is clear that this censure can have no reference to a dying man, who can no longer benefit anybody, and can only make his friends suffer with himself. While, therefore, we utterly repudiate the saying of Madame de Staël (in one of her earlier and less matured writings), that suicide is an " acte sublime," and while we may consider that such men as Clive, Condorcet, and Prévost-Paradol incurred a grave responsibility in extinguishing talents which belonged to mankind, we may yet think that nothing but good could follow from the permission of euthanasia. There is another point which the Archbishop's saying suggests. Mr. Williams has striven to defend the morality of a certain form of suicide. It would, I conceive, much strengthen his case, and give, so to say, a second string to his bow, if proof could be forthcoming of what I would term the *legalisability* of suicide in general. Now, suicide, however immoral in most cases, seems to be one of those acts which relate primarily to their authors, and which the State has no power to check. Will it be said that suicide, if permitted, would extend its effects beyond the individual, since it would propagate itself by example? Of course it would, and so would idleness, and every vice under the sun. But the idle or frivolous man or woman is allowed to spread the infection of idleness and frivolity all around. The drunkard wears out his own constitution, and is of but doubtful profit to his neighbours; yet even he (so long as he only tipples at home) is unrestrained either by the Legislature, or by private individuals with the Legislature's sanction. Who then has a right to coerce that less objectionable member of society, the would-be suicide? If we may not interfere with the do-nothing-eat-all (or even drink-all), how can we meddle with the do-nothing-eat-nothing?

But it will be said that we are, at any rate, bound to restrain, not only "delirious" persons, but also such as are in an extreme "state of excitement or absorption," and that under one or other of these heads nearly all suicides will fall. I am aware that the amiable perjuries by which juries have sought to evade the provisions of a monstrous law, together with the natural wish of the suicide's friends that he may not even now be partaking of the hapless lot of impenitent sinners, have led many persons to the convenient conclusion that nearly all suicides are mad; but there is, unfortunately, only too much evidence the other way. Of course, a large proportion of suicides consists of persons who have suffered from great mental depression, and between depression and madness it is not always easy to draw a line. Still, for practical purposes, such a line has to be drawn constantly; and, under the new system, it would probably be recognised that a man who was sane enough to make his will, was sane enough to decide how soon the will should begin to take effect. A man, however much out of health, so long as he is not under restraint, should be regarded as the best judge of his own happiness; just as, if his friends wished him to occupy himself, they could not, even for what they deemed his good, make him work against his will. In any such case, the old saying about the gods may be paraphrased thus: *invalidi felicitas invalido cura*. Indeed, it may perhaps be doubted whether, when a man has seriously determined to commit suicide, his friends, even if able to stop him, always benefit him by doing so; for, to a man who has once fallen into this unhappy state, length of days is often an increase of sorrow. On this last point Mr. Williams is explicit with a vengeance. He declares emphatically, in language which makes part of his essay as doleful as a Scotch sermon, that suffering is the almost constant rule in nature; and he seems to apply the rule to every animal, rational or irrational, sick or in health, past, present, or to come. In assuming this principle, he employs an instrument quite sharp enough to cut the knot about euthanasia. But, unluckily, it will cut other knots equally well. If pain is always in excess of pleasure, was not Tamerlane one of the greatest of human benefactors? And, even if a general massacre is not the only consistent end of utilitarianism, is it not in all cases most immoral to bring children into the world?* I think, however, that it may be assumed—and the existence of society must involve the assumption—that the prospects of most healthy men are rather happy than the reverse; or, at any rate, that they will be so when the poor are better cared for. But it by no means follows that the balance is likely to be favourable in the case of men who wish to destroy themselves. There is yet another point to be considered. Lucretius exhorts old men to welcome

* Unless we resort to the rather fantastic hypothesis that our children are likely to deduct from the mass of human misery a greater amount than they will themselves feel. It is certainly remarkable that Mr. Williams's lugubrious opinion is in some measure supported by such writers as Herodotus, Plato, Cicero, Shakspeare (if, as M. Taine thinks, the poet is expressing his own sentiments in Hamlet's soliloquy), Milton, Bishop Butler, Byron, and Shelley. In like manner, Sydney Smith, shortly before his death, told Charles Austin that life seemed to him "a very middling affair." It is also singular that, if you ask a number of persons whether they would live their lives exactly over again, the majority will almost always reply in the negative: this probably is so,

death philanthropically, on the ground that nature wants the matter of their worn-out bodies, in order to make of it young and healthy bodies. And, in a somewhat similar spirit, modern science informs us that in an overcrowded population there is a sharp struggle for existence: so that an unhealthy, unhappy, and useless man is in a manner hustling out of being, or at least out of the means of enjoyment, some one who would probably be happier, healthier, and more useful than himself. Perhaps it will be thought that I am now on dangerous ground, since arguments not unlike the foregoing might be urged in defence of the Spartan custom of destroying weakly children. Yet, in truth, the two cases differ widely. The great and crushing objection to so atrocious a usage as infanticide is to be found in its extreme liability to abuse, and in the anti-

partly because many are misled by contrasting too strongly the shortcomings of their past life with what that life might have been, and partly because the recollection of pain is so intensely vivid that people cannot realise that they are supposed to enter on their renewed life, fresh, vigorous, and foreknowing nothing. The oddest case that I know on the other side is that of a kindly old Indian officer of past eighty, whom I asked whether he would like to live his life over again. "Live it over again!" he answered; with an enthusiasm of which I had thought him incapable, "I would live it five times over again. There is not a single day that I regret." As the Frenchman said, *C'est la façon dont le sang circule.*

social consequences that might follow it. It is possible that, under such a system, full-grown sons might sometimes turn the tables on their aged parents, and inquire concerning them what, not long ago, a young child asked an elderly relative, namely, whether " it would not soon be time for her to go to heaven." Occasionally, even, an impatient kinsman or heir might adopt a summary method similar to that which was so frankly avowed by Porphyria's lover:—

> " All her hair
> In one long yellow string I wound
> Three times her little throat around,
> And strangled her. No pain felt she;
> I am quite sure she felt no pain."

But there is, in fact, the same sort of difference between infanticide and suicide as between wasting one's neighbour's goods and wasting one's own. Either form of wastefulness is immoral; but bystanders would regard the one form as the waster's own concern, while with the other they would feel bound to interfere.

Would, however (it is asked), the Spartan father be alone, if euthanasia were permitted, in holding a power liable to abuse? Would not the authority which it is proposed to grant to the doctor be almost equally intolerable, though exercised over a willing subject? Without dwelling on the power over life and death which is exercised by home secretaries and commanders-in-chief, I may remark that even now the issues that depend on a physician's fallible judgment are often most formidable. For example, in the performance of the painful duty of rejecting as incurable applicants for admission into a hospital, the slightest error of judgment will take from those that have not, whatever chance of getting better they might seem to have. In the case of euthanasia, the doctor would merely have to say whether the sufferer was in such a state that, had he wished to enter a hospital, the request would have been refused. If further precautions were required, the concurrence of two or three medical men might be held necessary for granting the sick man a release from his sufferings. Something of this sort might be done if Mr. Williams's demand, and nothing more, were conceded. But, if the legal right of suicide were once fully recognised, the matter would become much simpler; for then the entire responsibility would lie with the sick man. This would be especially valuable in cases where there was a certainty of long and acute pain, and a probability, just short of certainty, that the pain would end in death.

"But, at any rate, would it not be the height of cruelty to quit one's sorrowing friends? And is not the State bound to protect them from such a base desertion?" When conviction for suicide involves loss of property—when social inconveniences attach to the suicide's relatives—when it is popularly held that all sane suicides will be damned,—when any of these conditions, having but lately ceased to exist, have left an after-glow of sentiment about the sacredness of life,—in all such cases (as also when the sufferer has insured his life) the friends are most careful to prevent him relieving his misery by a *coup de grâce* of any sort. Yet nothing is more certain than that it is not by the mere fact of the sick man's dying that so much sympathy is aroused; for, after prolonged suffering, the friends will nearly always speak of death as a merciful release. And I suspect that among the poorer classes, unless the sick man happens to be a pensioner, the equivocal affection which would wish him to linger on in agony would give way yet sooner before the labour of nursing him.* But, be this as it may, we may cut the matter short by repeating the substance of our former question: Has the

* This may be illustrated by an anecdote concerning a well-disposed husband in that class. His wife, dying of asthma, had been troubling him, in the intervals when she could speak, with directions of all sorts. He struggled hard with his impatience, and at last said quietly, "Dinna fash yourself, my good woman, but get on with the deeing."

State any right to forbid the sick man to choose his own way of severing himself from his friends, when it cannot possibly prevent him ordering (as in *Middlemarch*) even his nearest relations to keep out of his sight?

I will conclude my duties, as self-chosen counsel for euthanasia, by adverting to two objections which have been urged by a very able, and by no means unfriendly, critic.* As I repeat the first of these objections from memory, I will give it entirely in my own words. " Granting that such a principle as that of the absolute sacredness of life cannot be logically defended, it is certain that the opinions and actions of most men are very little determined by logic. Men are often deterred from committing atrocious crimes by traditional sentiments, which are the result of very complex associations; and with these sentiments and associations it is dangerous to meddle. Thus, the duty of respecting one's own life, even in extreme cases, is a sort of outwork, by surrendering which we should much imperil men's respect for each other's lives; at any rate, it is safe policy to insist on the less obvious duty, for by doing so we obey the proverb, and *take care of the pence.*" I have already touched on this subject in what I have said about infan-

* *Saturday Review.*

ticide; but, as the objection is by far the most serious that can be urged against euthanasia, I will now consider it more fully. In trying to meet this difficulty, the first point that strikes one is, that we can see but a short distance into the future of history, and that, therefore, if we rejected all reforms which might lead to contingent and remote evils, no reform whatever would be passed, and we should be in a state of Chinese stagnation. If Luther had foreseen all the consequences of the right of private judgment, he would, perhaps, never have quitted Rome. Nor is it merely ungenerous and cowardly to refuse reasonable concessions, lest they should be followed by unreasonable demands; it is often, also, unsafe. To revert to the two illustrations that I have just employed—there is sometimes a danger to the fortress in seeking to defend too long an indefensible outwork; just as there is a danger in being penny-wise. And, in the present instance, if the masses are taught to regard a proper respect for human life as involving a wanton prolongation of the death-agony, the logic may one day prove to be two-edged, and the association of the ideas to be a perilous one. Once more: soldiers, after a long and bloody campaign, come home, not perhaps with their moral sentiments much quickened or ennobled, but still without any propensity to pillage or shoot their peaceful neighbours. Why is all this bloodshed so little demoralizing? Undoubtedly because it has occurred in the name, and under the protection, of the law. Now, under the proposed scheme, the case of doctors, so far as it would differ from the case of soldiers, would differ from it for the better. For the doctors would be acting under legal sanction; their conduct in each case would be liable to public criticism; while, on the other hand, it would be comparatively seldom that they would have to shorten life, and, when they did shorten it, their motives would be the very kindest. Indeed, it may well be doubted whether less harm would not be done both to the doctors and to the public by the former being allowed to grant the incurable sufferer a willing release, than by their looking passively on, and often even using their skill to lengthen his pain. Will it be said that they also use their skill to relieve his pain, especially at the last stage? They do so, often by giving strong narcotics; but, as I have said, when narcotics, withheld before, are given when there is no longer any hope, it may be surmised that their probable effect will be that of, to say the least, not adding to the dying man's few remaining hours. Need I say, that if a doctor, even at an agonized patient's entreaty, takes a course likely to hasten death, he is doing that for which, under the present law, he might be severely taken to task; nay, that he is hovering on the brink of manslaughter, if not of something worse? And, granting that human life would be much more and much oftener curtailed, if euthanasia were allowed, than is now the case, is it not yet possible that there may be less danger in a considerable curtailment, when legalised and exposed to public scrutiny, than in a far smaller curtailment, when brought about irregularly, and, as it were, by stealth?

The other objection urged by the same critic is of less consequence. Speaking of euthanasia, he says :—

"The only answer which could be made from the point of view of practical convenience was the extreme liability to abuse of such a power. Dead men tell no tales; and it would be unpleasantly easy for a wife who wanted to get rid of her husband, to put an end to the unfortunate person's existence, and to set up the theory that she had acted only by the express desire of the invalid. There can, however, be no doubt that, if such a system could be introduced with sufficient safeguards, it would put an end to a great quantity of suffering."

While agreeing cordially with this last sentence, I would venture to suggest that safeguards could be multiplied *ad libitum*. Why should not precautions be taken similar to those which are required in order to put a lunatic under restraint?

It might be held requisite that the doctor should always be present at the final scene; and, if that was not a sufficient safeguard, the law might provide that a given number of respectable persons (say householders) should be witnesses, including, perhaps, some policeman or magistrate. Why should it not be part of the recognised duty of the incumbent of the parish to be present? The notion may seem whimsical; but Sir Thomas More suggests, in sober earnest, that the priests, instead of merely witnessing such acts, should actively encourage them. I see that Mrs. Crawshay refers to the passage; but it certainly deserves to be quoted, representing as it does the opinion of one of the ablest of men and most devout of Christians:—

"When any [Utopian] is taken with a torturing and lingering pain, so that there is no hope, either of recovery or ease, the priests and magistrates come and exhort them, that since they are now unable to go on with the business of life, and are become a burden to themselves and to all about them, so that they have really outlived themselves, they would no longer nourish such a rooted distemper, but would choose rather to die, since they cannot live but in much misery; being assured that, if they either deliver themselves from their prison and torture, or are willing that others should do it, they shall be happy after their deaths; and, since by their dying thus they lose none of the pleasures, but only the troubles of life, they think they act not only reasonably in so doing, but religiously and piously, because they follow the advices that are given them by the priests, who are the expounders of the will of God to them. They that be thus persuaded, finish their lives willingly, either with hunger, or else die in their sleep without any feeling of death. But they cause none such to die against his will, and they use no less diligence and attendance about him, believing this to be an honourable death. Else he that killeth himself before that the priests and the council have allowed the cause of his death, him as unworthy either to be buried, or with fire to be consumed, they cast unburied into some stinking marsh."

NOTE.

In reprinting my article on Euthanasia, I am anxious to guard against one of the many misconceptions to which I have been exposed. Some excellent persons seem verily to imagine that I wish—nay, expect—Sir Thomas More's project to be proposed during the next session, and straightway carried through Parliament. Such is assuredly not my expectation; nor is it my desire. Mr. Mark Pattison has hinted at the possibility that the despised Comtist may, two centuries hence, be more formidable than the dreaded Catholic; and, in like manner, my main object is to suggest that, after the lapse of an equally long period, the Euthanasian pioneers may have defeated their Athanasian antagonists. It will, peradventure, be objected, that neither the Editor of the *Spectator* nor myself (unless, indeed, some news of this wretched little world is sent to disquiet us in the Elysian fields) can ever satisfy our curiosity as to the Euthanasian proclivities of posterity; and that, therefore, my speculation is an idle one. I think not. Those of us who are convinced that the ultimate triumph of democracy is *bestimmt in Gottes Rath*, find that the conviction changes the attitude which we assume towards the democracy of to-day; and, in the same sort of way, if the "stream of tendency" is making for Euthanasia, or, at least, for an increased indulgence to suicide in general, we may hope that at no distant date public opinion will be modified in regard to suicide *in extremis*. Such a hope was entertained by so cautious a thinker as the late Mr. W.

R. Greg, who represented himself as "wild about Euthanasia," and who (so far as I could judge from a single conversation) was both a more sanguine and a more vehement champion of the cause than I ever was. A similar hope or wish is expressed in the following extract from the memoirs of the great musical composer, Berlioz, to which a friend has called my attention:—

"J'ai perdu ma sœur ainée. Elle est morte d'un cancer au sein, après six mois d'horribles souffrances qui lui arrachaient nuit et jour des cris déchirants. Mon autre sœur qui s'était rendue à Grenoble pour la soigner et qui ne l'a pas quittée jusqu'à la dernière heure, a failli succomber aux fatigues et aux cruelles impressions que lui a causé cette lente agonie. Et pas un médecin n'a osé avoir l'humanité de mettre fin à ce martyre en faisant respirer à ma sœur un flacon de chloroforme. On fait cela pour éviter à un patient la douleur d'une opération chirurgicale qui dure un quart de minute, et on s'abstient d'y recourir pour le délivrer d'une torture de six mois. Quand il est prouvé, certain, que nul remède, rien, pas même le temps, ne peut guérir un mal affreux; quand la mort est évidemment le bien suprême, la délivrance, la joie, le bonheur! .... Mais les lois sont là qui le défendent, et les idées religieuses qui s'y opposent non moins formellement. Et ma sœur, sans doute, n'eût pas consenti à se délivrer ainsi si on le lui eût proposé. 'Il faut que la volonté de Dieu soit faite.' Comme si tout ce qui arrive n'arrivait pas par la volonté de Dieu. .... et comme si la délivrance de la patiente par une mort douce et prompte, n'eût pas été aussi bien la volonté de Dieu que son exécrable et inutile torture. .... Quel nonsens que ces questions de fatalité, de divinité, de libre arbitre, &c. !! C'est l'absurde infini, l'entendement humain y tournoie et ne peut que s'y perdre. En tout cas, la plus horrible chose de ce monde pour nous, êtres vivants et sensibles, c'est la souffrance inexorable, ce sont les douleurs sans compensation possible arrivées à ce degré d'intensité; et il faut être ou barbare ou stupide, ou l'un et l'autre à la fois, pour ne pas employer le moyen sûr et doux dont on dispose aujourd'hui pour y mettre un terme. Les sauvages sont plus intelligents, et plus humains."

THE FEAR OF DEATH.

"O! genus infelix humanum, talia divis
   Cum tribuit facta atque iras adjunxit acerbas!
   Quantos tum gemitus ipsi sibi, quantaque nobis
   Volnera, quas lacrimas pepercre minoribu' nostris!"
                                                    LUCRETIUS.

Is the fear of death less or greater in modern than in ancient times? In seeking to answer this question, we may say roughly that the physical terrors of death are constant, while the moral terrors are variable. Not, indeed, that the mere physical terrors have been, strictly speaking, unchanged. For it is probable that the ancients, being used to hardship and suffering, were less sensitive to the sting of death than we are. On the other hand, it is certain that the progress of medicine, including the use of anæsthetics, has done something towards extracting that sting, and will in time do much more. No doubt, our medical improvements often increase the immediate fear of death which is felt by the dying: if the dying suffered more, their minds would be distracted, and they would shrink less from the final relief. But, at any rate, those medical improvements tend to mitigate the apprehension which the mere pain of dying excites in the world at large. And it is enough for my purpose that this pain of dying can hardly be worse with us than it was with our forefathers; the balance, if balance there is, is probably in our favour.

Yet, strange to say, the entire terrors of death seem to be greater in our time than in that of the great classical writers. To prove this assertion would not be easy; but scholars will hardly dispute it. It is remarkable that Bacon, when maintaining the paradox that the fear of death is the weakest of emotions, chooses all his examples from among pagans. He mentions, among other instances, the dying jest of Vespasian: *Ut puto, Deus fio*. It would be unfair to judge of the ancient indifference to death from this exceptional utterance; just as, on the other hand, it would be unfair to judge of the modern alarm at death from the case of Johnson, who, when the surgeon made slight scarifications in his swollen leg, exclaimed, "Deeper; deeper! I want length of life; and you are afraid of giving me pain, which I do not value." Yet it is hard not to think that these opposite frames of mind exhibit the ancient and modern tendencies in regard to death, though they exhibit them "writ large." The best of the ancients knew, as we do not know, how to obey the maxim of the great poet of Stoicism, and to

D

take a negative view of death as the mere end of life, the goal in the course of nature; if infirm or suffering, they could even go the length of Juvenal's maxim, as rendered by Dryden—
" And count it nature's privilege to die."

Hence they managed to take death easily, through thinking of it as a matter of course, and thinking but little of it even thus; while with us, on the other hand, death is just what Byron called it— "the doom we dread, yet dwell upon"; and it is life which now dwindles into being the accident of our existence—*l'antichambre de la mort*,* or rather, *de l'éternité*. In truth, the ancients (or, more properly, the Greek and Roman free citizens), in seeking *fortem animum, mortis terrore carentem*, acted by anticipation on Charles Austin's rule, not to regret the inevitable; and to this unregretfulness, this dislike of breaking their wings against the bars of their cage, they owed much of that light-hearted joyousness which formed a real side of their character, though a less important side than we are apt to think.†

It is observed by Lessing that, in comparing

* Dumas.
† No passage in Herodotus strikes me as more impressive than the one (vi. 98) in which he says, that in the three generations which had just elapsed, more evils befel Greece than in the twenty generations before. He is speaking of the age of Miltiades, Themistocles, and Pericles—the very

the views entertained by different ages or races concerning death, their art proves a safer guide than their literature. Perhaps we may explain the grounds of this judgment by saying that literature is able, and is therefore expected, to give a diorama of what it depicts, while art can give only a panorama. Thus, in describing death, writers, especially poets, have to ring the changes of ever-varying, yet monotonous, details concerning the "groans and convulsions, the blacks and obsequies that shew Death terrible." On the other hand, a painter or sculptor is in the strictest manner bound to the unities of space and time. Thus, if he seeks to represent death in the abstract, he can only give a momentary and concentrated view of it. His representation must (so far as it goes) include everything, and yet must include nothing that needs to be explained; so that he must confine himself to the essential and

greatest, and, one would have thought, happiest age in the annals of the greatest and happiest nation of antiquity. Also he himself seems to have been a happy man; happy certainly in this, that he was born and died just at the right time: he was a child when Greece became safe from Persia, and his long life closed before the fall of Athens. Yet this great and happy man, speaking of this great and seemingly happy age, could only describe it as eminently miserable. The fact is, that he had a near view of the age, while we only see it "foreshorten'd in the tract of time." What is this historical perspective worth?

constant features of death, as distinguished from those which are accidental, and which vary in individual cases. What, then, are the essential ideas of death that are embodied in ancient and in modern art? To this Lessing replies, that ancient art generally symbolizes death by emblems of repose and insensibility — modern art by a skeleton. It is true that he deprecates and denounces this tendency of modern art. Being himself *on the side of the angels*, he would have agreed with Coleridge that a good man's surest friends should be " himself, his Maker, and the angel Death." And as an angel, rather than as a skeleton, he would fain have seen death typified. Still, in dealing with things, not as he wished them to be, but as they are, he emphatically declares that ancient art and ancient thought represented death more favourably than modern art or modern thought. Hence it appears that his authority in this matter, being given with reluctance, should carry all the more weight, and that this authority is distinctly on the side of the view for which we have been contending.

Assuming, then, that the entire terrors of death have increased, while its physical terrors have, if anything, diminished, what has increased must be the aggregate of its non-physical, or, as we call them, its moral terrors? What, let us ask, is the nature of these moral terrors? Some of them are of minor importance, being indeed little more than a reflection of the physical terrors. Thus, Mr. Mill at one time condemned capital punishments on the ground that, by connecting death with crimes, they add an imaginary to the natural horror of it; much as King John, apologising to Hubert for unflattering comments, improved matters by explaining that a suspicion of murder had "presented thee more hideous than thou art." Probably, however, we should be on our guard against expecting (in later life Mr. Mill would hardly have expected) men's nerves to be much strengthened by any mere mechanical reform like the one I have mentioned. Yet there is at least one such reform which might do some good in this direction: the aspect of death might be a little softened, if cemeteries gave place to *crematories*, and our minds were relieved from the revolting associations of the grave. If cremation has such a tendency, some of the ancients had, in this respect, less inducement to fear death·than we have. Also, it may be contended that, if the ancients had little fear of the end of life, this may have been partly because they set little value on the beginning or middle of it,—the difference between them and us being, not that they dreaded death less, but that we love life more. This remark may have some application to Orientals, both present and past : as, for instance, we may gather from the gloomy view of life expressed in the Dravidian hymns of India. But the explanation can scarcely be extended to the free citizens of the great classical nations; for, granting that, in spite of appearances, our life is happier and brighter than theirs was, it certainly cannot be so much happier and brighter as to set in appreciably greater contrast the dark colours of death. Moreover, some Orientals must have had a special reason to fear dying, particularly the Buddhists, whose posthumous ideal for the best of us is, that we must, through much tribulation and many transmigrations, enter into the land of nothingness. Yet Buddhism is not the only or the chief religion which, through the *post mortem* mystery, has the effect of attaching men to life. Christian charity, it is true, has done much to make the domestic ties tender and sacred; and this is one reason why we shrink so much from dying, and leaving those who will grieve for us. But Christian charity is not the only cause of our so recoiling from the separation. It might have been thought that the Christian faith, by declaring the parting not to be final, would do as much to mitigate its pang as Christian charity could do to embitter that pang; yet, in fact, Christian faith and Christian charity seem to combine to embitter it. The pain of the final parting, as felt by Christians, is partly due to the deep solemnity which Christian sentiment attaches to death; and this solemnity is not unconnected with a vague sense of dismay at the tremendous uncertainty as to what our dying friends will see and feel when their eyes are closed. In short, there is reason to think that it is "the dread of something after death" which now makes cowards of us all; and that, St. Paul notwithstanding, Christian mourners, as a rule, have sorrowed, not less than others who have no hope, but more than others who have no fear.*

Let us consider those beliefs further. Children, says Mr. Max Müller, help to correct the irregularities of language. They also set in a strong light, and so help to correct, the more flagrant

---

* Probably, also, the modern development of the primitive belief that, without shedding of blood, there is no remission, and the momentous results attributed to the death on Calvary, have helped to give a direction and an intensity to the Christian sentiment about death. Observe, too, that a moderately good Pagan might hope to be moderately happy hereafter; whereas a moderately good Christian, or rather Protestant, is tottering between infinite extremes, without even purgatory to serve as a mean. The paths of two men, whose degrees of sinfulness differ by a hair's breadth, may diverge into torment and glory: *ille crucem pretium tulit, hic diadema.*

anomalies of belief; and therefore it is interesting to observe the impression which the popular creed produces on their unsophisticated minds. Some time ago, a relative of tender years startled me by the question whether I should dislike going to hell. On my expressing displeasure at so singular an inquiry, the child explained, with equal simplicity and point, that, as most people would go to hell, surely he or I, or one of his parents, or of his brothers and sisters, must be of the number.* As to the condition in which the poor child expected some of his kinsfolk to spend eternity, I may refer to a hymn which used to be sung in a parish church, and which was taught to me in my boyhood. The following verse remains in my memory, after the lapse of twenty years; for it most happily illustrates the orthodox doctrine which, more than any other, took possession of my youthful mind:—

> "When I hear the wicked call
> On the rocks and hills to fall;
> When I see them start and shrink
> On the fiery deluge brink;

---

* The fear of hell takes various, and sometimes grotesque, forms; as was shown in the story of the dying Scotchman, who asked his minister whether he could save himself from the wrath to come by leaving £10,000 to his kirk. "I canna promise that," said the shrewd theologian, "*but it's worth trying.*"

> Then, Lord, shall I fully know,
> Not till then, how much I owe."

This ghastly thanksgiving falls little short of a saying attributed to some noted Evangelical: "Mr. Maurice doesn't believe in the eternity of punishment, but *we* hope for better things." In the following lines from another hymn, the sentiment is peradventure less encouraging, because it replaces gratitude with fear:—

> " Satan is glad when I am bad,
> And hopes that I with him shall lie
> In fire and chains and dreadful pains."

Some centuries ago a learned divine pronounced that "Beati in regno cœlesti videbunt pœnas damnatorum ut beatitudo illis magis complaceat." In a like spirit, a rigid Covenanter said that " the greatest delight of the saints in heaven will be to look down into hell and see the damned folks grill"; and, so recently as 1839, the sentiment found a feeble echo in the statement that "the beholding of the smoke of their torments is a surpassing delectation."* One of Lord Palmerston's bishops discoursed on the supposed difficulty of people being happy in heaven, while knowing that their deceased kinsfolk were else-

---

* See *Pall Mall Budget*, March 24, 1877.

where. In heaven, he explained, sympathy with the will of God will be indefinitely strengthened; at the same time, ties of family will be weakened: so that, instead of pitying our doomed relatives, we shall actually take part with the divine justice which dooms them. Perhaps it will be contended that the authority of a mere Palmerstonian prelate is worth little or nothing; so my next extract shall be from a prelate of real weight, the author of *Ductor Dubitantium* and of *Holy Living and Dying* :—

"We are amazed to think of the inhumanity of Phalaris, who roasted men alive in his brazen bull: this was a joy in respect of that fire of hell, which penetrates the very entrails of the body without consuming them. .... Such are the torments and miseries of hell, that if all the trees of the world were put in one heap and set on fire, I would rather burn there till the day of judgment, than suffer, only for the space of one hour, that fire of hell. .... Who would not esteem it a hideous torment, if he were to be burnt alive a hundred times, and his torment was to last every time for the space of an hour?—with what compassionate eyes would all the world look upon such a miserable wretch! Nevertheless ... what comparison is there betwixt a hundred hours' burning, with some space of time betwixt every hour, and to burn a hundred years of continual torment! and what comparison will there be betwixt burning for a hundred years' space, and to be burning without interruption as long as God is God!"

Observe that Jeremy Taylor here understands the texts about the *fire* of hell in their plain and literal sense. His example was followed by a Calvinistic clergyman who, some years ago, was guardian to an unconverted young lady. The late Sir Benjamin Brodie assured me that this too zealous pastor and master, after deliberating how he could best give his ward some slight foretaste of the posthumous discomforts that were in store for her, came to the conclusion that feeling is believing, and held her finger in the candle! On hearing of this *argumentum igneum*, one is tempted to think that either the guardian was mad, or else the story is exaggerated. I will, therefore, follow it up with another story, which reached me on equally good authority, and which is in itself less improbable. Quite recently, an orthodox parson was asked by one of the farmers in his parish whether he really believed that hell-fire would last for ever. He shrugged his shoulders, and quoted some of the texts which support the popular belief. "But, Sir," said the perplexed rustic, "I don't see how any constitution could stand it." This physical objection may recall one that occurred to a very old woman who, being admonished to beware of the place where there will be gnashing of teeth, drew comfort from the reflection that she had no teeth to gnash. Baden Powell has somewhere recorded three views which were taken by great Catholic authorities as to the existence of Antipodes. St. Augustin declared the belief to be unscriptural; Lactantius pronounced it to be absurd; while Boniface said that there might indeed be Antipodes, but that they would all without exception be damned.

Alas! how often one has thought that, on the first day of Creation, if benevolence had really been armed with omnipotence, the *fiat* would have been, not " Let there be light," but " Let an infinite number of sentient beings be perfectly happy for ever."

Of course it is not meant that these dismal doctrines have ever been fully realised by a large number of persons; otherwise the case put by Bishop Butler might occur, and whole districts might go mad. Yet, in all probability, the "darkness visible" has really been more visible than we are apt to think; and especially it has been seen by the thoughtful and inquiring. The Puritans, with their glimmering light, were more disturbed by it than the Catholics were; and, if orthodoxy stands still while investigation goes forward, the evil is likely to be an increasing one. The bracing intellectual air that we now breathe will bring the latent diseases of our religion out. It will become more and more difficult for reflecting persons to hold the popular creed without partly realising it, and without the realisation making them miserable.*

Indeed, it is no mere supposition, but an historical fact, that the "glad tidings" of orthodoxy are tidings the most appalling that ever exercised a great influence; under no other system has there been so intense and widespread a belief in future torments, themselves so intense, general, and prolonged. But from this historical fact some of the earlier Utilitarians, including more than one eminent historian, drew a hasty generalisation; for they would have given—the historian of Greece, with his classical sympathies, would especially have given—an echo to Béranger's prophecy or prayer that the sceptre would depart from the creed which deposed Hellenism, and that the God of Olympus would be avenged on the God of Zion:—

* This opinion, as well as some others that I have expressed, is confirmed by Mr. Mill, at the end of the essay on the *Utility of Religion* (pp. 115-122), which I did not see till the text of my article was finished. I venture to think that, in other parts of that essay, he makes too little of the distress arising from the popular belief. It is true that pious relatives, whose son or brother has died either in immorality or in unbelief, seldom think it *probable* that he will be damned. But I am certain that they often find it hard to drive away the thought that the unpleasant contingency is *possible*. Indeed, unless their nerves are in a much better condition than their heads, or else than their hearts, this could scarcely be otherwise.

"Déjà meurt l'école nouvelle ;
Déjà Satan baille et s'en va ;
Viens, Jupin, du haut de l'échelle
Voir dégringoler Jéhovah."*

Indeed, that grave and admirable historian (as reported by Charles Austin) maintained that "the success of Christianity was one of the greatest calamities that ever befell the human race"; the reason assigned being that the belief in hell, by embittering the fear of death, has "cast a gloom over modern life." It may serve to set forth our own view of the limits and results of the fear of death, if we offer in conclusion two remarks on this more extreme view, and on the antichristian iconoclasm which some followers of the great Bentham founded upon it. In the first place, one may regard the belief in hell as having embittered the fear of death,—and yet be, in no sense, an iconoclast. For, through long usage, the moral conduct of most men is at present so dependent on theological dogmas, that those dogmas may be

* This unedifying stanza may be instructively compared with language which is sometimes used by sound divines with reference to orthodox opinions which they themselves do not happen to hold. Thus, Dr. Arnold, when asked whether he believed in a doctrine which the majority of Christians regard as an essential part of Christianity, answered that he had rather worship Jupiter. After all, would it not be a less evil to worship Jupiter than to worship the God of Calvin?

likened to the supports of a lame man, and should only be withdrawn by slow degrees, here a little and there a little; otherwise, the national morality, stripped too suddenly of its religious bandages, might realise Mr. Greg's forebodings, and fall; and great would be the fall of it. It would, indeed, be an odd application of my remarks on moral courage,* if I concluded with a panegyric on our British cowardice in expressing, nay, in holding, unpopular opinions. Assuredly, we should be better off in many ways if we could put a speedy end to our intellectual anarchy and illogical compromises. Yet a comparison of the present state of the different European countries may reconcile us to the thought that our divines play the part of a spiritual House of Lords, and ratify, however slowly and ungraciously, the changes which "the common-sense of most" forces upon them. That they will act thus in regard to the belief in hell, we may infer from their concessions in other directions. In divers departments of knowledge, a reformer, by this time, knows what to expect. The first generation of theologians will execrate him; a later generation will try to ignore him; while a third will stand aghast at the judicial

---

* This article should be read in connection with *Physical and Moral Courage* (in *Safe Studies*), of which it was originally the sequel.

blindness which so long overlooked the scriptural foreshadowings of the new discovery.* This is not very pleasant for the reformer; and, if he does not say in his haste that all clergymen are untruthful, he will at least be tempted to rail at their vicarious penitence in "building the sepulchres" of the philosophers, whom their fathers persecuted. Yet, when his railing fit is over, he will probably think that we should congratulate ourselves on the elasticity of modern dogmas, and especially on what I lately heard a Catholic priest denounce as *la souplesse du Protestantisme*. Many evils, such as the theological disunion of the sexes, are mitigated by the fact that divines follow lay inquirers, though at a respectful distance, and that science, as it were,

---

* To give an instance: I have heard a highly instructed clergyman argue from the Bible in favour of the antiquity of man, and of the original plurality of human races. For, with whose aid, and for whom, did Cain build a city? Also, whom did he marry, being an outcast before the birth of his sisters? My friend omitted to state whether it was by means of swimming that the non-Adamites survived the Deluge; which of us, not being sprung from Adam, are free from original sin; and how little pain women, that are not daughters of Eve, have in childbirth. In like manner, the Pauline epistles contain, at least, two Universalist texts, which, however much opposed to other texts, are quite enough for liberal theologians. I may add that there is a text sanctioning the principle of Euthanasia (at least for persons of good family): 2 Maccabees xiv. 42, *et seq.* Not only "doth the

takes religion in tow. Therefore, the wiser among us are seeking to drop hell out of the Bible as quietly, and about as logically, as we already contrive to disregard the plain texts forbidding Christians to go to law, and Christian women to plait their hair. And thus we may hope that, without any cataclysm in the theological strata, but by a gradual process of subsidence and upheaval, a change will come over those too consistent Puritans who, through fear of death, are all their life subject to bondage.

Our other comment on the Benthamite position is of a wholly different kind. It is by no means clear that the modern *strepitus Acherontis avari*, however silly and distracting, has on the whole been injurious. The teaching of the clergy, though in itself not good, may yet, as the clergy would express it, have been overruled for good. It would, no doubt, be far better that the path of life should be a mere *cul de sac*, than that it should lie on the brink of an unseen precipice. But it is not, on that account, an evil that man should at one time have believed in this precipice. The error may have been the only means of

Church read" this book "for example of life and instruction of manners," but (as Alford admits) it is recognised as an authority in the Epistle to the Hebrews. How long will Euthanasia be thought unchristian?

inducing him to set the example of treading warily, and to smooth the path for his successors by taking stumbling-blocks out of their way. In other words, Christianity has made the human race less imperfect through suffering. If men at first became sadder, they became also wiser; and they showed their wisdom in trying to lessen sadness. They that are whole, says the Scripture, have no need of a physician; and, without an exaggerated view of human depravity and misery, our forefathers might have lacked the stimulus for repentance and reformation. At any rate, having the stimulus, they repented and reformed in a way in which the pagans, not having the stimulus, did not repent and reform. Hence, looking to the past, we may rejoice that, not *L'Allegro*, but *Il Penseroso* is the man whom Christianity delighteth to honour; and that, instead of the pagan *Carpe diem*, her watchword is *Memento mori*.

FEARLESS DEATHS.

"Il faut vouloir vivre et savoir mourir."
                                   NAPOLEON.

IN our last paper we endeavoured to show that Christianity has tended, not to mitigate, but to increase the terrors of death. An objection to this view may be drawn from the depressing stories that are current about philosophers' death-beds. In order to meet this objection, it seems necessary to give some examples of philosophers whose dying moments were conspicuously without fear. We give these examples with reluctance, because of the affectation with which some of them are disfigured. Yet even from this affectation something may be learnt. By its very exaggeration it sets in a stronger light the painful, yet withal playful, acquiescence—the *horrible joie*, as Edmond Scherer has called it—with which some dying men have contrasted the permanence of natural forces with the decay of everything that lives, and have concluded that human life, with all its strength and beauty, is a tragi-comedy ending in a bathos. The nearest approach to such a sentiment that we have ourselves experienced was when the *Spectator* proclaimed that, according to Mr. Proctor, a comet seemed to meditate striking the sun, and that it was in nowise impossible that in fifteen years (the exact term of prolonged life assigned to Hezekiah) all life on our planet might be destroyed. However improbable it appeared that so overwhelming a calamity would be thus casually announced for the first time, it came sufficiently home to us to enable us to form an estimate of the manner in which such a catastrophe, if really impending, would affect us. And we own that what most impressed us was a sense of the irony of the universe: we thought we should feel (if the fatal concussion were imminent) that we had all been serving our fellows and Art and Science and Mammon for naught; that Charles Austin's great wish was about to be realized; and that, not by an act of destructive vengeance, but by the agency of natural laws, we should attain a speedy Euthanasia. In short, we were thrown into sympathy with Shelley's couplet:—

> "The world is weary of the past:
> Oh! let it die and rest at last;"

but we were yet more disposed to exclaim, *Si foret in terris, rideret Democritus.* Perhaps, after all, this sentiment is not wholly unlike that of Charles Lamb, who with grim humour professed to lament.

that Guy Fawkes had not succeeded in blowing up the House of Lords—it would have made such a sensation in history!

Having premised thus much, we can now address ourselves to the question: How far are philosophical death-beds exceptionally marked by fear? In dealing with this subject, two considerations suggest themselves. We may remark, in the first place, that a modern freethinker, who, with great suffering, has "obtained this freedom," is not like a thinker who is "free-born." Those who (as Tennyson puts it), "after toil and storm, may seem to have reached a purer air," seldom shake off the effects of the less pure air and the fatigue; and they are apt, especially in their last hours, to be haunted by the impressions of their youth, and the beliefs of those around them. This tendency of dying persons was well indicated by Patru, when Bossuet visited him on his deathbed. "Monsieur," said Bossuet, "on vous a regardé jusqu'ici comme un esprit fort. Songez à détromper le public par des discours sincères et religieux." "Il est plus à propos," replied the dying man, "que je me taise; on ne parle en ses derniers moments que par faiblesse ou par vanité." The enervating effects of training up a child in the fear of hell are especially visible in the pupils of those austere Calvinists, from whose early influence it is so hard to release oneself, and who expect the kingdom of heaven to be about as populous as the princedom of Monaco. Secondly, the true account of a heretic's death-bed is often hard to obtain. Sometimes, as in the case of Voltaire, his enemies persuade others, and perhaps themselves, that he actually felt what they expected him to feel, and his remorse is evolved out of their own consciousness; sometimes, on the other hand, they give a flippant version of his courage, and distort it in a cynical caricature. The latter cause may have helped to produce the stories about Rabelais. It said that, when dying, he sent for his domino, with the words, "Beati qui in Domino moriuntur." When Cardinal du Bellay sent his page to inquire after him, the dying man replied: "Tell your master the state you find me in; I am going in quest of a Great Perhaps. He is up in the jay's nest. Bid him keep where he is; and, for you, you will never be anything but a fool. Draw the curtain; the farce is ended."

In an old work by Deslandes, several instances are related which bear on this subject, and some of which closely resemble the anecdotes just given. It is there stated that Gassendi, in his last illness, exclaimed: " I know neither who placed me in the world nor why I was placed in it, nor why I am taken from it." This uncertainty recalls the stanza of Omar Khayyam:—

> "Into this Universe, and *Why* not knowing,
> Nor *Whence*, like Water willy-nilly flowing;
> And out of it, as Wind along the Waste,
> I know not *Whither*, willy-nilly blowing."

There is more of hopefulness, or rather of playful fearlessness, in the answer of Heine, who at the close of his long agony was asked whether he shrunk from death: *Dieu me pardonnera, c'est son métier.* A similar calm was shown by Landor, who in extreme old age wrote the lines:—

> "Death stands above me, whispering low
> I know not what into my ear:
> Of his strange language all I know
> Is, there is not a word of fear."

Some years before, he wrote on his seventy-fifth birthday the following more famous stanza:—

> "I strove with none, for none was worth my strife,
> Nature I loved, and, next to Nature, Art;
> I warmed both hands before the fire of life,
> It sinks, and I am ready to depart."

Chateaubriand, when dying, at the age of eighty, during the lamentable revolution which overturned Louis Philippe, used words in which Mr. Arnold discovers the note of a rich and powerful nature:—" Mon Dieu, mon Dieu, quand donc, quand donc serai-je délivré de tout ce monde, ce bruit; quand donc, quand donc cela finira-t-il?" One used to be taught at school that, if the proportion of oxygen in the air were much increased, we should all die from excess of joy. Something approaching to this condition seems to have fallen to the lot of W. Hunter, who gave death a hearty (we had almost said a *swanlike*) welcome. His dying exclamation was: " If I had strength enough to hold a pen, I would write how easy and pleasant a thing it is to die." It is said that the last words of Hobbes were: " I am going to take a great leap in the dark." Shortly before dying, the English sage exhibited his wit; after rejecting various epitaphs suggested by his friends, he said he should prefer the inscription, " This is the philosopher's stone." He thus almost realised beforehand the important part of the ideal of Charles Lamb, who hoped that his own last breath would be inhaled through a pipe, and exhaled in a pun. Sometimes a more or less witty flash of indignation is struck out of a dying man by the obtrusiveness of theological busybodies. A Frenchman in his last illness, being thus wearied by a priest, silenced his ghostly importuner with the promise: " Vous serez payé, mais laissez-moi en repos." The famous Grammont, shortly before he expired, received a visit from the Marquis de Dangeau, who was sent by the King to try and convert him.

The dying man, though in agony, could not forbear twitting his sorrowing wife, who was *dévote*, with the suggestion that the Marquis might succeed in doing what she had long sought to do in vain: "Comtesse, si vous n'y prenez garde, Dangeau vous escamotera ma conversion."* Bourdelot, being troubled in his last moments by a priest who used great plainness of speech, implored him to veil his coarse exhortation in Latin. In compliance with this whim, the astonished *curé* proceeded to quote St. Augustine — "Quoi! monsieur," interrupted the penitent, "pouvez-

---

* One is a little, but only a little, less shocked by this flippancy when one reflects on the quaint protests sometimes made by pious Catholics whose prayers have been (so to say) *overanswered*. At Capri there is a saintly old woman who is believed to have great influence with the Powers above. After a long drought, she was persuaded to offer up a petition for rain. Her "effectual fervent prayer" availed overmuch; and the result or sequel was a deluge. When the next drought occurred, she was again requested to pray, but this time to pray less earnestly! The request showed a childlike desire to limit the bounty of the *Di faciles*. The same desire may be illustrated by an anecdote of a wholly different kind. An English lady informs me that, when she was a young girl, she went into the Madeleine under the escort of an elderly duenna. In the church she observed that a Frenchman who was in love with her was saying his prayers. She is convinced that he had no thought of being irreverent when he presently came up and said to her: "J'ai bien prié de vous voir à l'église, Mademoiselle, et vous voici. *Mais il paraît que le bon Dieu m'a mal compris, puisque je n'ai point demandé la vieille.*"

vous approuver un pareil langage? Mon oreille est choquée des expressions rudes d'un Africain." Some French Pyrrhonist, when making his will, is said to have begun it thus:—"At my death, if I am now alive, I leave my soul, if I have one, to God, if there is one." Vanini, when about to be burnt at Toulouse on the charge of atheism, exclaimed in a clear voice: "Jésus-Christ a, dit-on, craint la mort; et moi, je suis intrépide en ces derniers moments."* It must be owned that this not very modest or conciliatory comparison savours somewhat of sensational display. A characteristic form of such love of display has been shown by certain French purists, whose grammatical pedantry haunted them through life, and who split hairs at their dying gasp. Malherbe—to whose influence over French poetry Boileau has paid a superb compliment,—when on his deathbed, rallied his last remains of strength to correct a bystander for an inelegance of diction; being

* Some examples of callousness on the part of condemned criminals are recorded by Montaigne:—"One that they were leading to the gallows told them they must not carry him through such a street, lest a merchant, that lived there, should arrest him by the way for an old debt. Another said to the hangman, he must not touch his neck for fear of making him laugh outright, he was so ticklish. Another answered his confessor, who promised him that he should that day sup with our Lord, "Do you go then," said he, "in my room, for I, for my part, keep fast to-day."—Book I. ch. 40.

rebuked by his confessor for this levity, he declared that he could not help himself, for he felt bound "défendre jusqu'à la mort la pureté de la langue Française." This may recall the story of the Academician whose life had been occupied with verbal subtleties, and whose dying words were— "Je *vais*—ou je *m'en vais ;* car l'Academie n'a pas encore decidé." We need hardly observe that this jocularity of moribunds nearly always rings hollow, and that it has little in common with genuine courage like that of the Normans, who (according to Gibbon) sighed in the laziness of peace, and smiled in the agonies of death. Indeed, in the two instances last given, the affectation is as evident, if not quite as offensive, as in the case of those who deliberately act a part in the last scene of their lives, and dress up for dying. Thus, when about to expire, Augustus Cæsar, after sending for a mirror and arranging his hair, asked jestingly whether he was not a good comedian; and, with a like bravado, Buchanan, though strictly forbidden in his fatal illness to drink wine, died nevertheless theatrically holding a glass in his hand and reciting verses of Propertius. Some of these details concerning philosophical death-beds may, we repeat, be doubtful. But, at any rate, there can be no doubt that death was met with ostentatious indifference by that not very philosophical patroness of philosophers, Madame de Pompadour. She put on a silk dress, and painted her face (like Pope's Narcissa); and, when her confessor was leaving her, she stopped him; "Attendez un instant, M. le curé; nous nous en irons ensemble." Her levity had a fit counterpart in the cynicism of her royal lover, who, on seeing her funeral procession, shed no tear (he had not the *don des larmes*), but merely exclaimed: "Madame la Marquise aura aujourd'hui un mauvais temps pour son voyage."* Such cases of apathy, whether on the part of the dying persons themselves or of their friends, may be given for what they are worth; but assuredly they ill contrast with the dignified fortitude which was shown by so many of the ancients, and which the ancient poet of annihilation has finely indicated:—

> "What horror seest thou in that quiet state,
> What bugbear dreams to fright thee after fate?
> No ghost, no goblins, that still passage keep;
> But all is there serene, in that eternal sleep."†

---

* In a like spirit, Butler alludes to the storms which accompanied the death of Cromwell:—
> "Toss'd in a furious hurricane
> Did Oliver give up his reign."

Dean Ramsay, in his tales of Scottish humour, relates that a pious Miss Johnstone, without a thought of irreverence, complained of the weather when she was dying—"Ech, what a nicht for me to be fleeing through the air!"

† Lucretius translated by Dryden.

This pæan over death has a special interest as exhibiting the pagan tendency even in one who, though *in* paganism, was not *of* it—who was what may be termed a pagan infidel. How strangely does his confident and defiant tone differ from the melancholy beauty of the following stanza by another infidel poet—an infidel, however, who was penetrated with modern sentiment, and on whom Christianity had left its mark:—

> " This world is the nurse of all we know,
>   This world is the mother of all we feel,
> And the coming of death is a fearful blow
>   To a brain unencompassed with nerves of steel:
> When all that we know, or feel, or see,
> Shall pass like an unreal mystery."

It is true that the same pathetic uneasiness had been shown long before by pagan writers. Adrian, for example, in his celebrated lines, reveals a similar disquietude. But, when he composed those lines, the world had already half gone over from Western strength, one may say, to Eastern tenderness; paganism was being undermined, not indeed by Christianity, but by those more general causes which predisposed men's minds to receive Christianity. Hence in Adrian possibly, as undoubtedly in Marcus Aurelius, the new spiritual forces are apparent which have wrought so powerfully on modern beliefs.

The view of the "glad tidings" of orthodoxy, and their results, which we have sought to establish in this article and the preceding one can scarcely be better summed up than by short extracts from three of the most distinguished writers of our day—writers whose authority is especially valuable, as two of them are Christians in sympathy, and as all three are, if not Conservatives, at least opposed to iconoclasm. In the *Life of Bunyan*, Mr. Froude writes: "Given Christianity as an unquestionably true account of the situation and future prospects of man, the feature of it most appalling to the imagination is that hell-fire — a torment exceeding the most horrible which fancy can conceive, and extending into eternity—awaits the enormous majority of the human race." Well may Mr. Lecky observe that, "of these doctrines it is not too much to say, that in the form in which they have often been stated [by the most famous divines], they surpass in atrocity any tenets that have ever been admitted into any pagan creed. . . . . Such teaching is, in fact, dæmonism, and dæmonism in its most extreme form." George Eliot is equally explicit :—

"Wherever the tremendous alternative of everlasting torments is believed in—believed in so that it becomes a motive determining the life;—not only persecution, but every other form of severity and gloom are the legitimate consequences. There is much ready declamation in these days against the spirit of asceticism and against zeal for doctrinal conversion ; but surely the macerated form of a Saint Francis, the fierce denunciations of a Saint Dominic, the groans and prayerful wrestlings of the Puritan who seasoned his bread with tears and made all pleasurable sensation sin, are more in keeping with the contemplation of unending anguish as the destiny of a vast multitude whose nature we share, than the rubicund cheerfulness of some modern divines, who profess to unite a smiling Liberalism with a well-bred and tacit, but unshaken confidence in the reality of the bottomless pit."

NOTE.

It must be owned that Lucretius represents an intense fear of death as prevailing among his countrymen. But Macaulay thought, probably with reason, that his statements are exaggerated. The exaggeration (if such it was) was no doubt designed as an excuse for the arguments with which he assailed his national theology, and which are so unfortunately applicable to other theologies that (in the delicious phrase lately used in Parliament) his poetry is " only less objectionable than Mr. Bradlaugh's writings."

The only classical writing, so far as I am aware, which represents the modern aspect of the fear of death, is the pseudo-Platonic dialogue called *Axiochus*. This dialogue, though written in late Greek, is undoubtedly pagan; it probably belongs to the time of which we have spoken, when paganism was giving way by reason, not of Christianity, but of " those more general causes which predispose men's minds to receive Christianity." The argument is briefly as follows: Axiochus, an old man on his death-bed, loses his nerve and sends for Socrates to comfort him, just as a dying Christian would now send for a clergyman. Socrates tries to console him with dialectical quibbles, such as that death has to do neither with the dead nor with the living. The poor old man complains that these subtleties are all very well for young men, but they are cold comfort in the hour of death. Thereupon, Socrates changes his theme, and assures Axiochus that his soul is merely escaping out of prison into a land where sorrow and old age will be replaced by a philosophic calm; and he adds a sort of apocalyptic myth, to the effect that after death the righteous will be received into Elysium, while the wicked will be removed to a place of torment where their devouring wildbeast dieth not and their fire is not quenched (λάμπασιν ἐπιμόνως πυρούμενοι ἀϊδίοις τιμωρίαις τρύχονται). On hearing these gladdest of glad tidings, the old man straightway casts aside his fear, and has even a desire to depart. It may be worth while to compare this singular dialogue, so far as it reveals the future of the righteous, with the famous epitaph in the Greek anthology, of which the subjoined hexameters are but a free and feeble paraphrase:—

Οὐκ ἔθανες, Πρώτη, μετέβης δ' ἐς ἀμείνονα χῶρον,
Καὶ ναίεις μακάρων νήσους θαλίῃ ἐνὶ πολλῇ·
Ἔνθα κατ' Ἠλυσίων πεδίων σκιρτῶσα γέγηθας,
Ἄνθεσιν ἐν μαλακοῖσι κακῶν ἔκτοσθεν ἁπάντων.
Οὐ χειμὼν λυπεῖ σ' οὐ καῦμ' οὐ νοῦσος ἐνοχλεῖ,
Οὐ πεινῇς, οὐ δίψος ἔχει σ'· ἀλλ' οὐδὲ ποθεινὸς
Ἀνθρώπων ἔτι σοι βίοτος· ζώεις γὰρ ἀμέμπτως
Αὐγαῖς ἐν καθαραῖσιν Ὀλύμπου πλησίον ὄντος.

Dying, thou art not dead!—thou art gone to a happier country,
And in the Isles of the Blest thou rejoicest in weal and abundance.
There, Protó, is thy home in the peace of Elysian meadows,
Meadows with asphodel strewn, and peace unblighted with sorrow.
Winter molests thee no longer, nor heat nor disease; and thou shalt not
Hunger or thirst any more; but, unholpen of Man and unheedful.

Spotless and fearless of sin, thou exultest in view of Olympus; Yea, and thy Gods are thy light, and their glory is ever upon thee."

May it not be said of these lines and of *Axiochus*, that they are (as it were) missing links between Paganism and Catholicism, and that their creed is Christianity without Christ?

DIVINE ECONOMY OF TRUTH.*

'Ὦ μή 'στι δρῶντι τάρβος, οὐδ' ἔπος φοβεῖ.
SOPHOCLES, O. T. 296.

"SUPPOSE," says Mr. Mill, "that certain unknown attributes are ascribed to the Deity in a religion, the external evidences of which are so conclusive to my mind as effectually to convince me that it comes from God. Unless I believe God to possess the same moral attributes which I find, in however inferior a degree, in a good man, what ground of assurance have I of God's veracity?"† In other words, if God's justice and mercy are not as our justice and mercy, what guarantee have we that his truth is as our truth? And, conversely, are not orthodox reasoners, who start with the assumption that God's truth is as our truth, likewise bound to assume that his justice and mercy are as our justice and mercy? We propose to discuss this question at some length; for it seems to suggest the most easily stated and, so to say, handiest reply to the

* *Fortnightly Review*, Dec., 1877.
† Professor Newman, I think, has said to the same effect:—
"If God may be what we should call cruel and unjust, why may He not be what we should call a liar?"

familiar platitude, that the only legitimate exercise of reason in these matters is to convince us of the reality of the Christian miracles, and that, being once convinced, we ought straightway to accept any doctrines, however seemingly immoral, which the recorders of those miracles have preached.

This subject has lately been brought under my notice by Father Oxenham's work on "Catholic Eschatology and Universalism." In that work the doctrine of eternal punishment is upheld; and it is not thought blasphemous to represent God as the author of hell. Yet the same work, referring to some one who has suggested that the accounts of eternal punishment in the Gospels may have been exaggerated for a moral end, pronounces that suggestion to be "little short of blasphemous." In short, God is too good to deceive, but not too good to damn. Now, if Mr. Oxenham were alone in maintaining this paradox, I should not be at the pains to controvert it; for, differing from him *toto caelo* (*totâque*, let me add, *gehennâ*), I feel that between him and me, except on some minor topics, there is no common ground for argument.

But, unfortunately, there are many Protestants and even nibblers at Liberalism who hold vaguely and perhaps unwittingly what this able writer has stated clearly and forcibly: it is mainly with these, and wholly for their sake, that my present discussion is set on foot. In fact, my article is a plea for that generally valuable yet generally unvalued body, the Neochristians—those transformed and regenerate Ishmaels, whose hand is against no man, though every man's hand is against them. And the motive of this plea is an earnest desire that the religious reform which is inevitable, should be kept as far as possible within the Christian lines. Still, a measure of reform which is to avail against revolution has often to be somewhat drastic; and the first advice which should be offered to our Neochristian friends is, that they should at once give up the old foundation, for which their modest structure is unfitted, and on which Pandæmonium may so easily be built. But, before entering on their defence, a word of personal explanation is required. Mr. Mill certainly held that a Being who could create hell would be, strictly speaking, not a "God," but the very reverse. Yet, in the chapter by him from which I have quoted, the popular language is repeatedly adopted for the sake of clearness; and to the supposed author of hell the name "God" is applied. In the present article that example will be followed. It will also be found convenient to assume, unless when the contrary is specified, that the Church is right in pronouncing certain writings to be genuine and certain marvels to be historical. But it must be understood that I am not bound by these assumptions. It should, moreover, be explained that, zealous though I am on behalf of the Neochristians, I in nowise commit myself to either of the recognised forms of Neochristianity,—either to Mr. Tennyson's Christianity without hell, or to Mr. Arnold's view, which, as Comtism has been called " Catholicism *minus* Christianity," may not unfairly be entitled " Christianity *minus* Theism." My position will be rendered yet clearer by my adding that I expect the various orthodox sects, with their chronic civil war, to continue in a state of heedlessness not wholly unlike that which the Gospel attributes to the antediluvian world: they will preach, they will write, they will cavil, they will give in to cavils, till science comes and destroys them all. Wherefore, of the Catholic and the orthodox Protestant it may be said, as of Lausus and Pallas, that neither is destined to overwhelm the other, but that *mox illos sua fata manent majore sub hoste.*

Doubtless, to satisfy Mr. Oxenham personally, the foregoing explanation was not needed; for he clearly thinks me an honest (if somewhat ravenous) wolf in wolf's clothing, and has even singled me out as the representative of the common enemy into whose hand timid or treacherous friends (seemingly Broad Churchmen) are playing. It is possible that the simplest way of opening our inquiry will be to quote and expand, from a former article, a passage from which he has made an extract. " The wiser among us," I said, " are seeking to drop hell out of the Bible as quietly, and about as logically, as we already contrive to disregard the plain texts forbidding Christians to go to law, and Christian women to plait their hair,"* or, it might have been added, to be unveiled in Church; bidding all Christians work miracles on pain of damnation;† bidding them choose psalms and spiritual songs as a vent for their mirth;

* P. 49.

† Mark xvi. 16–18. Nothing can be more arbitrary than the way in which orthodox Christians, especially Protestants, make *v*. 16 refer to *all* believers, *v*. 17–18 only to *some*. The plain sense is this: "Who will be saved? Only believers. How are believers to be recognised? By their miracles." Compare the reproachful tone of Matt. xvii. 17–21, where it is clearly implied that the miraculous power was to be perpetual. In Acts ii. 17–20, St. Peter (misquoting Joel) expressly states that this power was to be abundant "in the last days." "Bunyan," says Macaulay, " was disturbed by a strange dilemma. 'If I have not faith, I am lost; if I have faith, I can work miracles.' He was tempted to cry to the puddles between Elstow and Bedford, 'Be ye dry,' and to stake his eternal hopes on the event." Of a not dissimilar state of mind some of us have had experience.

forbidding them to jest;* to take judicial oaths; to hope for exemption from " persecution "† (in the plain sense which the early Christians attached to that word); to receive interest for loans, or even to receive back the principal;‡ to be rich, or to ask rich people to dinner;§ to receive an unorthodox person into their house, or even to wish him " God speed." That this last prohibition was meant literally is proved by the tradition about St. John and Cerinthus; and I have heard an Evangelical divine, only too plausibly, adduce the passage to prove the sinfulness of entertaining Catholics. That some of the other texts I have referred to were not meant literally, is commonly and conveniently assumed. Personally, I could never take this view—not even in my orthodox boyhood, when such texts made life a burden to me; so that my judgment was then vehemently biassed, not against; but in favour of, the traditional interpretation of them. That the literal meaning of each of those passages is the true one, still seems to me probable. At any rate, it is certain that, taken collectively, they

* Eph. v. 4. Cf. Matt. xii. 36.
† 2 Tim. iii. 12.
‡ Luke vi. 34, 35. These and the other texts against usury were taken literally, until the needs of civilisation refuted them.
§ Luke xiv. 12, 13.

breathe an ascetic spirit which is in glaring contrast to the smooth and polished Christianity of our day. A popular preacher, complaining of Rationalists that they had no moral standard, once said to me, "When I am in doubt, I refer to my Bible": almost as if his Bible was unlike other Bibles; certainly as if the Bible was a lucid Encyclopædia of doctrine and morals. Nor did my friend herein go far beyond what is held by most orthodox Protestants. They have forged a vast shield of texts, which they use to their own satisfaction against Romanists (*Ingentem clipeum informant, unum omnia contra Tela Latinorum*);* and wherewith they hope to quench the fiery darts of the combined wicked—of Romanists and Rationalists together. Our object, on the other hand, has been to show that the Bible is not such a handbook as they suppose; and that, in fact, if the way of doctrinal transgressors is hard, that of Bibliolaters is not easy. And if, consciously or unconciously, orthodox Christians exercise the right of "dropping" inconvenient texts "out of the Bible," they should not be wroth with their Liberal brethren who do likewise; for the game, in very truth, is one at which two can play. Here, then, is our point:—If the Bible contains plain commands which we have a

* Æn. viii. 447.

right to disobey, may it not contain plain assertions which we have a right to disbelieve?* Thus the Neochristian would be in no lack of orthodox precedents if he contended that the statements about hell were Oriental hyberboles; or that they were an extra deterrent mercifully given to the Jews in their low state of piety, or rather of culture and civilisation—an adaptation to the hardness of their hearts, or perhaps to the softness of their brains; or that they were a needful concession to a prevailing superstition: for the Bible was written *a Judæis, ad Judæos, apud Judæos;* and superstition, like nature, *non nisi parendo vincitur.* Nay, further: the Neochristian may express his view by a phrase which has lately been invented, or rather revived, by orthodox divines; for he may maintain that such an accommodation to human ignorance as I have just indicated is not, strictly speaking, deceit; it is merely a judicious husbanding (οἰκονομία) or "economy of truth."

Perhaps, indeed, it will be objected that our

* Mr. Justice Stephen says (*Liberty, Equality, and Fraternity*, p. 315) that some scriptural commands are "understood by those who believe in the supernatural authority of Christ as a pathetic overstatement of duties .... peculiarly liable to be neglected." Every argument that can be used to justify such a "pathetic overstatement" of duties, will serve to justify a pathetic overstatement of the penalties whereby those duties were enforced.

analogy between disobeying Divine commands and disbelieving Divine assertions does not hold. Let us, then, give an example of each kind. It is plainly declared that the observance of the Sabbath—an observance binding in regard to the day, the obligations, and the penalties—was to be "perpetual," and "for ever."* And this perpetual ordinance, originally imposed on Israel, extends to all who have adopted Israel's law.† It is also affirmed that the "house," "kingdom," and "throne" of David should be "established for ever." Compare these two statements with the statement that hell is to be perpetual. If, by a prophetic license, *perpetual* means *transitory* in regard to the Sabbath and the House of David, why not in regard to hell? Or (what is much the same thing), if we may give a non-natural interpretation to two of these propositions,‡ why not to the third?

Impartial readers will probably think that I

---

* Ex. xxxi. 16, 17. † Matt. v. 18. Cf. Matt. xxiv. 20.

‡ Thus, it is commonly maintained that the throne of David spiritually survives in Christianity. To test this interpretation, let us put a parallel case, which we can consider impartially. One was told at school that Virgil's *Imperium sine fine dedi* is a signal instance of an uninspired prophecy failing. Yet it might be at least as plausibly urged that the Roman dominion survives in the Papacy, as that the Davidic throne survives in Christianity. But, to any such pitiful misinterpretation of Virgil's words, a sufficient

have already made out my case; but, as the subject is very important, and as the prejudice about it is inveterate, I will carry the inquiry somewhat deeper. To reasonings like the above it is commonly objected that (according to the Bible) God can neither "lie" nor "repent." Now, it is obvious that this objection is at once refuted by the fact that it proves the biblical veracity from the Bible, making the Bible arbiter in its own cause. But I will let this pass, as I wish as far as possible to meet orthodoxy on its own ground: ἐκ τοῦ στόματός σου κρινῶ σε. The Bible, then, asserts that God neither lies nor repents. But, in the very same chapter,* God is described as repenting: hence it might be argued that the biblical statement on this head, so far from proving that there are no biblical mis-statements, adds to their list one mis-statement the more. But this difficulty also I will not press. An orthodox person would probably meet it by

answer would be that, before the Roman Empire ceased, no one dreamt of so explaining the poet's meaning. Even so we may ask, Did the Jews, before the time of Nebuchadnezzar, dream of spiritually *evaporating* the plain prediction about David?

* 1 Sam. xv. 11, 29. In this singular chapter a still more startling contrast occurs: Samuel (*v.* 22) expresses the noble sentiment that "to obey is better than sacrifice"; yet, at that very moment, he was meditating the most hideous of all sacrifices—a human sacrifice (*v.* 33).

saying that the Divine word, like nature, half reveals and half conceals the soul within; we can see God only through a glass darkly, or rather through a pseudoscope,—*immortalia mortali sermone notamus;* hence there is no inconsistency in supposing that God does not really repent, but that to our finite reason He can only be revealed as repenting. Well, let this explanation stand; only let us observe that in the Hebrew verse—that *rime de pensées*, as M. Renan calls it—"lying" and "repenting" are coupled together. The Divine incapacity of misrepresentation is announced in the same breath, and placed in the same category, with the Divine incapacity of repentance. And yet, humanly speaking, God *does* repent. Is it, then, impious to inquire whether, humanly speaking, God may not misrepresent? Nay, further: according to the only notion that we can form of repentance, a repentant man must either err when he repents, or have erred in doing that for which he repents. Surely this reasoning, *mutatis mutandis*, applies to a repentant deity. Perhaps an illustration will best set forth our meaning. We are told that God repented of the good work of creating man. Therefore, his beneficent decrees do not resemble the laws of the Medes and Persians. Why, then, must we assume that his maleficent decrees resemble those laws? If it repented God of creation, may it not repent Him of the intention of damnation?

But it is not only out of the Bible that eternal punishment is defended. The burden of proof is attempted to be thrown on the assailants of that doctrine. The doctrine, it is said, is rendered antecedently probable by the analogy of nature. In nature the wages of sin accumulate till death; a sinful act never ceases injuriously to affect the sinner; but whatever occurs in nature must be permitted, if not ordained, by God; and the presumption is that his supernatural government bears some analogy to his natural; and, therefore, that the punishment of sin, which has no end in this world, will likewise have no end in the next. Now this reasoning, which is substantially that of Butler, could not be fully examined without discussing the argument of the first chapter of the "Analogy," and even the fundamental assumption on which the "Analogy" rests. This is not the place for such a discussion: so I will merely remark that natural forces are in themselves neither moral nor immoral, but *outside morality;* but, when they are personified and judged by a moral standard, they are found to be recklessly immoral.* Hence, if

---

* "La Nature," says Renan, "est d'une immoralité transcendante."

we start with the assumption that the course of nature is in harmony with God's direct and deliberate action, we may go on to defend the foulest superstition that ever cursed mankind. If whatever exists (including Nero's government*) is "ordained of God," theft and adultery must be so ordained. If, then, God's natural procedure is a sample of his supernatural, what right have Christians to condemn the actions attributed to Jupiter, which were, humanly speaking, immoral? Nor is it only civilised Jupiters, ancient or modern, that may claim the benefit of such a plea. The plea is equally applicable to those "puny godlings of inferior race" † whom savages worship, nay, even to Bhowanee, the goddess of murder. Hence, when Shelley indignantly denied that—

> "The God of nature and benevolence had given
> A special sanction to the trade of blood,"

his indignation was partly reasonable, partly not. That the God of benevolence should have sanctioned such a trade, is, of course, impossible; but that the God of nature, the ordainer of all the abominations that occur in nature, should have done so, is in nowise impossible, but just what we might have expected. Nor, again, are we left to

* Rom. xiii. 1. † Dryden's *Persius*.

conjecture as to the employment of the analogical aid to faith in support of religious systems which we now justly condemn. On the contrary, we know that, when pagan orthodoxy was giving way, such pagans as Plutarch and some of Lucian's interlocutors propped it up with arguments not unlike those wherewith the disciples of Butler now prop up Christian orthodoxy. So that, after all, Butler's and Mansell's sanctuary is a too Catholic Pantheon—a veritable "shrine of all saints and temple of all gods"—where mutually destructive theologies seek a common refuge.* It is, however, with such attributes as those of Hermes Dolios that we are specially concerned. If it was God who hardened Pharaoh's heart, we may assume that it is often, if not always, God who hardens the liar's heart; in every such case *Deus fallit per alium;* analogy, therefore, points to the presumption that some-

* If we first realise the undoubted fact that the competing religions, *certificated* as they all are with prophecies and miracles, stand, as regards external evidence, practically on a par,—if we then carry out Mansell's argument to the extent of disabling human reason from criticizing, and therefore from distinguishing between, the relative strength of their internal evidence,—all external and internal evidences will be eliminated, and all the systems will be reduced to a dead level. Why, then, should we choose one rather than another? Should we not have to exclaim with Celsus— Οὐδὲν οἴομαι διαφέρειν Δία [*i.e.* Θεὸν] Ὕψιστον καλεῖν, ἢ Ζῆνα, ἢ Ἀδωναῖον, ἢ Σαβαώθ ?

times *Deus fallit per se.* But this is not all. That the sun travels from east to west, that the earth is approximately a flat surface, that the blue sky is a solid vault (στερέωμα)—these are delusions which the plan of the universe has done its very best to foster, which are common to primitive races, and which primitive writers, inspired as well as uninspired, have emphatically shared.* In the face of these delusions, will the paradox that the course of nature is a representation, however imperfect, of the Deity—a not inglorious "mirror where the Almighty's form glasses itself in" moral "tempests,"—be seriously maintained? If so, we are driven to the monstrous conclusion that there are qualities in the First Cause little akin to those of Nathaniel,—

* In a curious passage of Herodotus (iv. 158), the Lybians, describing a place with a great rainfall, say that ἐνταῦθα ὁ οὐρανὸς τέτρηται, almost as if the firmament leaked and needed a plumber. In Bachr's note this expression is compared to Gen. vii. 11 ; it might have been compared to a yet more important text, Matt. iii. 16. The plurality of the "heavens" is affirmed in the first clause of the Lord's Prayer (comp. 2 Cor. xii. 2). The word is correctly translated in the Vulgate (*caelis*). May not the progress of scientific knowledge be discerned in the passage as translated in the A. V. ? May not that progress be also discerned in our Authorized rendering of Ezek. v. 5, a passage cited by Ewald as shewing that the Jews (like the Greeks) regarded their own country as the centre of that circular plain, the world (*Hic est Jerusalem, in medio gentium posui eam et in circuitu ejus terras*—Vulg.) ?

that (if I must needs be plain) the heavens declare the mendacity of God and the firmament sheweth his unfaithfulness. And hence would arise the analogical presumption that, in revelation, God (according to St. Paul's happy euphemism) "calleth those things that be not as though they were."

Xenophanes blames Homer for attributing to the gods—

ὅσσα παρ' ἀνθρώποισιν ὀνείδεα καὶ ψόγος ἐστίν . . .
κλέπτειν μοιχεύειν τε καὶ ἀλλήλους ἀπατεύειν.

In this strikingly modern passage two things may be noted. First, divine deceit is not put in a class by itself; it is merely ranked with other forms of divine guilt. Secondly, the various forms of divine guilt are pronounced to be such, only on the assumption that the Gods are bound by human morality; the acts are condemned because they would be deemed " wrong and disgraceful among men." Now, it must be owned that to create millions of sentient beings, foreknowing that most of them were doomed to eternal tortures, compared with which the perpetual extraction of a sensitive tooth would be hailed as a relief *—such an act is unlike those which are thought praiseworthy among men. Are

* I give this realistic comparison in order to bring home to my readers what the popular doctrine is. People who talk glibly about *glad tidings* should read (in Wall's *History of*

we not, then, bound to blame this act when imputed to God? For, in truth, there are two standards, and only two, whereby acts so imputed can be judged: there is the standard of human morality, and there is the immoral standard of natural analogy. Almost always, in weighing Christian and non-Christian theologies, we play fast and loose with these two standards. Will it be said that Christianity is in itself superior to the best non-Christian theology? It is; but we vastly exaggerate the superiority by applying to the different theologies different tables of weights and measures. The divergence between these tables far exceeds what is commonly supposed. Weighed in the balance of natural analogy, *no* historic gods are found wanting; weighed in the balance of human morality, *all*.* The like may be said of the comparison between damning and

Infant Baptism) Augustine's and Fulgentius's expressions about the fate of unbaptized (including stillborn) infants. It is, however, satisfactory to know that, although Augustine (once at least) explicitly declared that all unbaptized children would be damned, yet he trusted that "this fire would be to them the most moderate of all" (Wall).

Likewise from Jonathan Edwards we learn that
"in bliss
They may not hope to dwell;
Still unto them Thou wilt allow
The easiest room in Hell."

* I use the phrase "historic gods" so as to exclude such deities as the Ormuzd of Plato, of Mr. Mill, and of those

deceiving. If God is wholly beyond the pale of human morality, we cannot guess whether He ought to damn or not to damn—to deceive or not to deceive. If, however, He is within that pale, we may conclude that (if omnipotent) He ought neither to damn nor to deceive; but that the guilt of deceiving is as dust in the balance when compared with the guilt of damning. I say "if omnipotent," for the following reason:—That a good spirit of limited powers might, in extreme cases, have to deceive his creatures, is just conceivable. In those extreme cases we might agree with Æschylus that ἀπάτης δικαίας οὐκ ἀποστατεῖ θεός. But that such a spirit should be one

"Wha, as it pleases best hissel,
Sends ane to heaven, and ten to hell,
A' for his glory," *

is utterly inconceivable and revolting.† The

Christians (including one of Mr. Oxenham's critics) who hold that God permits no evil which He can possibly prevent. But it must be born in mind that every such Ormuzd has a supplementary Ahriman, and that, at bottom, every such system is Bitheism.

* Burns.

† If Ahriman had made Hell a necessary condition of creation, Ormuzd would not have created. "It had been better not to have given the earth unto Adam; or else, when it was given him, to have restrained him from sinning. For what profit is it for men now in this present time to live in heaviness, and after death to look for punishment?" (2 Esdras vii. 46, 47.)

orthodox, however, take a view the opposite of ours; they virtually assume that the text, "Let God be true, but every man a liar," is itself true in a more literal sense than the text, "God is love." Indeed, to their *apotheosis* of veracity may be due some of the exaggerated commonplaces that are current as to the absolute universality of the duty of truth-telling.* I remember, when a boy, being told that it was sinful in Napoleon to encourage the Guard at Waterloo with the misstatement that their comrades, having crushed Blucher, were in sight coming to help them. Yet it certainly seemed that to tell the Guard a lie for which, if it had succeeded, they would have been grateful, was, at worst, what Sophocles would have called ὅσια πανουργεῖν, and Shakespeare would have called "a virtuous sin"; and that, at all events—in judging of that long crime, Napoleon's career—

* This tendency probably reached its height in the philosopher who, as represented by Bentham, "says there is no harm in anything in the world but in telling a lie; and that if, for example, you were to murder your own father, this would only be a particular way of saying he was not your father." This erratic view of parricide may be incidentally compared with the one ascribed by Herodotus to the Persians. "They maintain that no one ever killed his father or mother; but that, whenever such an act was reported, it would inevitably be found on inquiry that the child was either supposititious or illegitimate; for (they say) it is not likely that one who was rightfully a parent would die by the hand of his own son."

to single out this peccadillo for reprobation, showed a want of moral perspective. But what should I have answered if my teacher had gone on to ask whether it was not uncharitable to suspect a man like Napoleon of telling such a lie? My answer would, or should, have been in the words of Œdipus. When Œdipus had adjured the unknown murderer of Laius to give himself up, the Chorus was so sanguine as to suggest that further efforts at detection would be needless; without doubt, the criminal, on hearing the imprecation, would make haste to confess his guilt. Whereunto the king rejoined: "Not he who dared the deed will shrink at words." We have prefixed this reply as motto to our article; for it happily exposes the delusion which prevails about the Divine morality. Whoever, in conceiving of that morality, strains at the gnat of even beneficent misrepresentation, while he swallows the camel of eternal punishment, should bind the motto about his neck, and write it on the table of his heart. But our popular teachers are deaf to such advice. They scorn to depict God as an idealized Edward III., pardoning those whom he had doomed to destruction; but they scruple not to depict Him as a Torquemada *in excelsis*. Indeed, it is not too much to say that, according to the popular estimate, the *splendide mendax* Hypermnestra is the only one of the Danaidæ whom God cannot be like. To show the justice of this last comparison, let us sum up the foregoing argument in theological language, after premising that, pursuing the Christian method of interpretation, we assume the sixth commandment to forbid all wanton cruelty, and the ninth to forbid all wanton deceit. Does, then, the moral law, as a whole, apply to God, or does it not? Or, if it be maintained that only part of it extends to God, how can we even guess which part so extends? If the ninth commandment, why not the sixth? If not the sixth, why the ninth? Nay, is it not more antecedently unlikely that a good being would break the sixth commandment than the ninth? How, then, can our finite reason presume to assert that, as regards the Infinite, *quod non probat minus probat majus* — that the lesser of these commandments is precisely the one that binds God, while from observing the greater of them He is dispensed?

But, after all, it is superfluous to show that, assuming orthodoxy, Divine deceptions may occur; Orthodoxy herself practically admits that they *have* occurred. How does she account for the scientific statements in the Bible, which are, to say the least, calculated to mislead? She affirms that those statements were needful accommodations: which being interpreted is, that God, to teach a great truth, had to teach a little error. But there are graver forms of Divine deception to which the Bible directly bears witness. Lucian justly complains that Zeus, in the Iliad, "deceived Agamemnon by sending him a lying dream, so as to cause the death of many Greeks." In exactly the same way, Jehovah, in the book of Kings, deceived Ahab by sending him a lying spirit, so as to cause the death of many Hebrews (*Deus fallit per alium*). At another time, He "gave them also statutes that were not good, and judgments whereby they should not live"; and "if the prophet be deceived when he hath spoken a thing, I the Lord have deceived that prophet" (*Deus fallit per se*).*

Nor is it only in the Old Testament that such deceptions are mentioned: they are attested also in the New.† I am careful to notice this latter testimony, inasmuch as it is on the earliest Christian traditions and sentiments — those recorded in the Synoptical writings and the Apocalypse—that the case for eternal torture chiefly rests. St. Paul, on the other hand, inclined towards Universalism;‡ and it does not lie with the Church to neglect his authority: for

---

* Comp. Deut. xiii. 3; Jer. xx. 7.
† 2 Thess. ii. 11. ‡ Rom. xi. 32.

ecclesiastical Christianity is based far more on the
Pauline Epistles and the Fourth Gospel than on the
genuine sayings of Jesus.* But St. Paul himself
would have been the first to disclaim any such
pre-eminence, and to admit that the servant is
less than his Lord. *Numquid Paulus crucifixus
est pro vobis? Aut in nomine Pauli baptizati
estis?* It is, therefore, with especial interest that
we inquire whether a strong case for eternal
torture can be made out of the language of the
Synoptical records. To me, their expressions
seem very strong: insomuch that, when Mr.
Oxenham holds up their damnatory phraseology
and virtually asks with Hubert de Burgh, " Can
you not read it? Is it not fair writ?" I most
reluctantly echo Prince Arthur's answer:

"Too fairly, Hubert, for so foul effect."

Not only is this concession in itself painful: it
also involves a painful inquiry. For it behoves
us to prove, not merely that there are errors in
the Bible—thus much all rational Christians now
admit,—but that there are errors even in the words

* It may be worth noting that St. Paul has exercised the same sort of nominally subordinate, but really paramount, influence over Christianity, as Chrysippus (himself, like St. Paul, a Cilician) exercised over the not wholly dissimilar system of the Stoics; insomuch that, just as it used to be said that "But for Chrysippus the Porch would never have been," so we may add, "Neither, but for St. Paul, the Church."

ascribed to the Master. Yet, in this thankless demonstration, it is a comfort to feel that we are only affirming a principle which all Neochristians practically assume, and which is indeed the corner-stone of their system; for it is certain that what may be termed the non-*populousness** and the non-eternity of hell are staked on the fallibility of Christ. From this point of view, then, all Christians, even those who *believe* our conclusions to be false, ought to *wish* them to be true. If a great physician told us that we were going to die of a lingering and loathsome disease, we should wish—he would expect us to wish, and would himself wish—that he might be mistaken; and so, when the Object of our deepest reverence has proclaimed sad tidings of great sorrow which are

* It is only fair to say, that Mr. Oxenham inclines to think that most men will not be lost. This question, of course, lies beyond the compass of a note. But I may remark that the words in Matt. vii. 13, 14, are as plain as words can be. If, then, it is "little short of blasphemous" to suppose that the Master used words calculated to mislead in regard to the duration of hell, is it much short of blasphemous to suppose that He used words calculated to mislead in regard to its populousness? And, on the other hand, if an orthodox Christian may virtually assume that in Matt. vii. 13, "broad" stands for "narrow," and "many" for "few," why may not a liberal Christian assume that in Matt. xxv. 46, αἰώνιον stands for ὀλιγοχρόνιον, or haply for οὐδεμίαν? To me it seems that the populousness and the eternity of hell rest on the same footing; and in this article they are classed together.

unto all people, common humanity bids us hope that even He was liable to error.

Before proceeding farther, I must guard against a misconception. Some readers may be estranged from this enquiry, through supposing that I am about to assail the doctrine of the Incarnation. Such, however, is not my intention; for, having a clear case before me, I mean to avoid all disputable matter. I will, therefore, remark that those who deny the infallibility of Christ do not *necessarily* deny his Divinity; they need only subject that Divinity to limitations which, in theory, are hardly greater than those to which it is subjected already. To make my meaning clear, I will first observe that in different ages the word "God" has been held to connote very different sets of attributes. Thus, Mr. Oxenham assumes that God is infallible; and, as we have seen, he thinks it blasphemous to suggest that the Incarnate God could deceive. Xenophanes, on the other hand, deemed it "blasphemous" to suppose that God could be incarnate at all;* whereas Hesiod saw nothing amiss in saying that the heavenly Muses " are skilled to tell many lies."† But it is not only in pagan authors that such representa-

* Ὁμοίως ἀσεβοῦσιν οἱ γενέσθαι φάσκοντες τοὺς θεοὺς τοῖς ἀποθανεῖν λέγουσιν.
† Ἴδμεν ψεύδεα πολλὰ λέγειν.

tions as this last are to be found. The Bible, we have shown, speaks of God as deceiving. In another place, God declares himself to be fallible, and even provides against the contingency of his having been misinformed.* Either this Divine statement is true, or it is not. If it is, *cadit quaestio*: if it is not, God is convicted of misrepresentation in this case, and capable of it in others. Of course, it may be contended that God is infallible in himself, but that, when speaking *down* to our faculties, He has to depict himself as fallible. I do not mean to contest this explanation; for, in conceding that God *as revealed to us* is fallible, it concedes all that my argument requires.

A different class of objectors may urge that God did not declare himself to be fallible, but was misrepresented by the author of Genesis. This solution, however, only throws the difficulty farther back: for the Founders of Christianity asserted, or rather assumed, the Divine authority of the Pentateuch;† so that, if the author of Genesis was mistaken, they were mistaken also. And this brings us to a remark about verbal in-

* Gen. xviii. 21. In 1 Kings xxii. 20-22, God is represented as at a loss for an expedient and as seeking counsel—in the art of deception.

† See Mark xii. 26. It is clear that the general state of opinion—the suppressed major premiss, as we may call it—

spiration. St. Paul believed in the verbal inspiration of the Old Testament.* Nor can there be any reasonable doubt that Jesus held the same view. Also, He promised his disciples that his teaching should be supernaturally brought to their remembrance; and that, when taken before judges, they should be verbally inspired.† These and similar passages serve to explain the desperate efforts that were made to defend verbal inspiration. In a work whose perfect accuracy is divinely guaranteed, even a minute error in fact involves a grave error in doctrine; for it proves that inspiration did not know its own limits. Extremes in theology sometimes meet; and I am glad to find that the views here enunciated may be confirmed by a quotation from Dr. Wordsworth. After rightly premising that the promise of verbal inspiration must be regarded as extending to St. Stephen, he goes on to comment on allegations that the proto-martyr's speech contains errors: "The allegations in question, when re-

which is involved in the assumption that the Divine words spoken in the burning bush were genuine, will cover the assumption that the Divine words confessing fallibility were genuine.

* Gal. iii. 16.

† Mark xiii. 11. How is this to be reconciled with Acts xxiii. 5? What would be thought of a modern witness who was affirmed to be infallible, but who, on entering the Court, failed to distinguish between judge and jury?

duced to their plain meaning, involve the assumption, that the Holy Ghost speaking by St. Stephen (who was 'full of the Holy Spirit') forgot what He himself had written in the book of Genesis, and that his memory is to be refreshed by Biblical commentators of the nineteenth century." This trenchant logic may be fitly coupled with Cowper's sneer at geologists, who

> "drill and bore
> The solid earth, and from the strata there
> Extract a register, by which we learn
> That He who made it, and revealed its date
> To Moses, was mistaken in its age!"

One has only to confront Dr. Wordsworth's logic with Alford's correct statement that St. Stephen's speech contains "at least two demonstrable historical inaccuracies"; and to confront Cowper's sneer with the first principles of modern geology; and one perceives what an edged tool every such *reductio ad anti-Christianum* is. But what concerns us is to note that, as we have said, rational Christians now-a-days admit that the Scriptures contain mistakes. Whence it follows that the Founders, who believed that the Scriptures (or large portions of them) were free from mistakes, were in that very belief themselves mistaken.

Moreover, the fallibility of Christ may be distinctly inferred from the Gospels. He is represented "as growing" (and therefore as at one time deficient) "in wisdom." He sought theological instruction from the Jewish doctors. Unless this instruction was a mere farce, He was then, if not fallible, at least inferior in knowledge to his fallible teachers. Also, in mature manhood, He knew not the day or the hour of his coming.* Hence his knowledge on some subjects was imperfect. And from imperfect knowledge to fallibility the step is a slight one; for, when a Being has imperfect knowledge, how can we be sure that his knowledge is perfect as to the limits of its own imperfection? But, as regards the fallibility of Christ, we are not left to mere conjecture. He "marvelled at the centurion's faith." Now, it is obvious that an infallible being could not marvel. When we say that a man marvels, we imply that his expectation fell short of the

---

* Mark xiii. 32. This and similar passages are explained away by some Catholics. Thus Pius IX. (quoted by Mr. Gladstone) has pronounced that Christ's increase in wisdom was "only apparent": whereunto a Neochristian might respond that future punishment will be "only apparent." So, again, the *Dublin Review* (September, 1865) says that "the Church imperatively requires her children to understand Mark xiii. 32 in some very unobvious sense." If the Church may take this liberty with plain texts in the New Testament, the Scribes and Pharisees (who sat in Moses' seat) must have had a like authority over plain texts in the Old Testament. Why, then, were the Jews blamed for giving a "very unobvious sense" to the Fifth Commandment (Mark vii. 9-13)?

reality, and was therefore erroneous. And thus, when we are told that Jesus marvelled at the centurion's faith, we infer that his previous estimate of that faith had been unduly low. Again: a Being conscious of infallibility would be free from doubt and misgiving. Yet Jesus was uncertain respecting his death; and, when dying, He feared that God had forsaken him.* In case this demonstration (for such it is) should be painful to any reader, I would fain offer a word of comfort. The great Catholic commentary of Cornelius à Lapide states that, "esto Christus non creverit sapientiâ et gratiâ habituali, crevit tamen actuali et practicâ." This reasoning is just as applicable to Christ's fallibility as to his youthful deficiency in knowledge; and hence a liberal Christian who clings to the belief in his Lord's Divinity, may plausibly urge that the Saviour (as was inevitable) held some errors of his time, but that in respect of those errors it was only his "actual and practical wisdom," not his "habitual wisdom," that failed him.

Having thus sought to disarm prejudice, we can more freely comment on a few out of the many erroneous statements reported in the Gospels —statements that may, as it were, keep in coun-

* Matt. xxvi. 39; xxvii. 46. See the *Note* at the end of the article.

tenance the reported statements about hell; and, in making the selection, we will mainly confine our view to errors that have been practically acknowledged by Christians of note. We will begin with an example that perplexed Mr. Maurice. The Master is said to have prophesied that He would "be three days and three nights in the heart of the earth." Now, the interval from Friday evening to Sunday morning is only one day and two nights. Hence, in the prophecy, as reported by St. Matthew, there is as open a breach with arithmetic as in the three fourteens in the same Evangelist's genealogy; and, we may add, as in his strange narrative (evolved out of a misunderstood prophecy) concerning the ass *and* the colt, on both of which (αὐτῶν) Jesus rode into Jerusalem.* Again, Jesus said that David ate the shewbread "in the high priesthood of Abiathar":† the event really occurred in the high priesthood of Ahimelech. Once more: an excellent religious journal has courageously proposed "to explain, once for all, that the theological and

---

* By the other three Evangelists, the supernumerary ass is suppressed. St. Matthew and the fourth Evangelist quote Zech. ix. 9 differently, so as to make it support their differing accounts. The fourth Gospel elsewhere furnishes a striking example of a myth *deposited* from a misunderstood text (xix. 23, 24).

† Mark ii. 26. I adopt Alford's translation, as the diffi-

historical library popularly called the 'Bible' contains some errors."* Now, the "error" that is chiefly referred to occurs in the Fourth Commandment. Did God give the Ten Commandments, or did he not? If he did, the "error" was a Divine one, and the thunders on Sinai were so many seals to that error. If he did not, the Master, who clearly believed the Decalogue to be from God, was himself in error on a fundamental point. The gravity of such an error may be best shown by an illustration. In the parable of Dives and Lazarus—that *tremendous parable*, as Charles Austin called it, which implies that all who receive their "good things" on earth, all whom a Jew of the Christian era would have counted rich, will be "tormented,"†—greater value is attached to the testimony of Moses and the Prophets than to that of one risen from the dead.‡

culty is slurred over in the authorised version. Alford comments on the instructive fact that a good and learned divine has persuaded himself that this text "rather suggests that he (Abiathar) was *not* the High Priest then": *nanum Atlanta vocavit, Æthiopem cygnum.* As for me, I forbear to waste words on the ingenious disingenuousness of harmonists: for I cannot even understand the notion that it is honest to apply to the Bible a mode of interpretation which would be dishonest if applied to any other book; and that orthodoxy, like Sigismund, is *supra grammaticam.*

* *Spectator*, August 28, 1875, p. 1091. † Luke xvi. 25.

‡ In like manner the writer calling himself St. Peter attributes greater probative force to the enigmatical pro-

Now, if one of the bystanders had suggested that one risen from the dead would appeal directly to the senses, whereas the passages in Moses and the Prophets (even assuming those passages to be genuine and rightly interpreted) might figure among the "errors" in "the theological and historical library popularly called the 'Bible,'"—if one of the bystanders (say the virtuous and enlightened St. Thomas) had suggested this, would not the remonstrance, "Be not faithless, but believing," have been the very mildest that would have been addressed to him? Again, not only did Jesus accept the entire narrative of the Pentateuch, but on the details of that narrative he founded important rules of conduct. In treating of the right of divorce, he appealed to the institution that was "from the beginning"; primitive institutions he assumed to be ideally the best. His reasoning suggests two reflections. First,—Whatever the primitive form of marriage was, strict monogamy it was not. Secondly,—The question as to primitive marriage, though indirectly full of instruction, has no direct bearing on conduct. As soon as science shall have determined how far primitive societies were endoga-

phecies of the Old Testament than to the evidence of St. Peter's own eyes and ears. (2 Peter i. 18, 19.) This tendency of the early Christian mind is suggestive.

mous or exogamous, modern communities will not be constrained to adapt their marriage laws to the primitive model: any more than those of us who believe slavery and cannibalism to have been primitive institutions, are therewithal bound to become slaveholders and cannibals.

These illustrations are given in no captious spirit, but in order to show how hollow is the truce that has been patched up between orthodoxy and modern research. Especially hollow is the truce between orthodoxy and Biblical criticism. For example: Jesus ascribed the 110th Psalm to David;* and the context shows that, in so ascribing it, he was not adapting himself to conventional phraseology, but that he thought that it was verily and indeed spoken by David. On the other hand, the "Four Friends" deny that it was by David; indeed, it was manifestly spoken not *by*, but *to*, a Hebrew ruler.† The "Four Friends," who write in a thoroughly Christian spirit, forbear to point the moral of their statement; but they can hardly have been ignorant

---

* Matt. xxii. 43, 44; comp. Acts ii. 34, 35.

† I say "ruler" (not "king") since there is a great difference of opinion as to when this psalm was written. It is stated in the *Psalms* by "Four Friends," that it was written during the monarchy; while our best Biblical critic, Dr. Davidson, is inclined to relegate it to the time of the Maccabees.

that, in making the statement at all, they were charging their Master with error. It is yet more obvious that their interpretation of the contemptuous apostrophe, "Ye are gods," is at variance with the amazing interpretation reported in the Fourth Gospel. Indeed, according to modern criticism, hardly one of the texts quoted from the Old Testament is rightly interpreted in the New. "Of prophecies in the sense of *prognostication*," says Coleridge, "I utterly deny that there is any instance delivered by one of the illustrious Diadoche whom the Jewish Church comprised in the name *Prophets*—and I shall regard *Cyrus* as an exception, when I believe the 137th Psalm to have been composed by David." In effect, this remarkable passage denies that the so-called Hebrew prophecies were predictions. On the other hand, Jesus believed them to be, not merely predictions, but predictions so plain that the Jewish nation was held guilty for not discerning their fulfilment. Thus, on so vital a question as prophecy, the opinion of the chief Christian philosopher of our century was diametrically opposed to the opinion of Christ. Other Christian writers follow Coleridge's lead. For instance: the Master is alleged to have foretold that a prophecy of Daniel was about to be fulfilled in the fall of Jerusalem, which was to be "immediately" followed by the end of the world.* Yet, not only has a certain interval already elapsed between the destruction of Jerusalem and that of the world; but we learn, even from Christian authorities, that the passage attributed to Daniel had no reference to the sack of Jerusalem by Titus—that it was not by Daniel—that it was not a prophecy, but a forgery. Hence, the book of Daniel furnishes a crucial test of rationalism. Laodicean liberals sometimes boast that they have given up their orthodoxy concerning the Old Testament, but that their orthodoxy concerning the New remains unimpaired. Now, if there is a point whereon rational critics from Porphyry to Zeller are agreed, it is that the prophecy in Daniel is unauthentic. If there is a point which lukewarm liberals are loth to give up, it is that every word of Christ came from God. To what, then, does their theory amount? Even to this shocking conclusion: that God professed to have inspired the pseudo-Daniel; and thus became accessory after the fact to a forgery. A similar mode of reasoning applies yet more directly to the theory of "inspired personation," a theory which seems to find favour with the accomplished divine who has written the article "Bible" in the *Encyclopædia Britannica*,

* Matt. xxiv. 15, 29.

and who has justly been described in a religious journal as the most orthodox of Biblical critics. That theory practically is, that the author of Deuteronomy, who was not Moses, was inspired to say that he *was* Moses (*Deo per mendacium gratificari*). Yet, peradventure, for this theory something may be said. We have seen that, on the orthodox hypothesis, St. Stephen's speech was verbally inspired. Yet, when professing to give the very words of Amos, he quietly substituted "Babylon" for "Damascus"; in fact, he manipulated the prophecy, so as to make it seem to have been fulfilled by the captivity.* It follows, then, that he was verbally inspired to misquote. If St. Stephen was inspired to misquote, why may not the Deuteronomist have been inspired to misreport?

But this is not all. A distinguished living clergyman told me that he considered the strongest passage in the Bible to be one where God, by the mouth of Jeremiah, disowned the entire ceremonial law.† The explanation of this

---

* Acts vii. 43. This practice was after the manner of the age. In Isaiah ix. 12, the LXX did not scruple to render "Philistines" by Ἕλληνες: their object being, according to a high authority, to make the prophecy refer to the Ptolemies and Seleucidæ.—See MACKAY's *Progress of the Intellect*.

† Jer. vii. 22.

passage probably is, that Jeremiah, like Ezekiel, felt that the Mosaic law contained statutes which, according to the moral standard of his own age, "were not good"; but that, whereas Ezekiel concluded that those unworthy statutes were given by God penally, Jeremiah more rationally concluded that they were not given by God at all. At any rate, Jeremiah's statement is incompatible with the divine authorship of the Pentateuch. How, then, is it to be reconciled with Christ's observance of the Passover, and his injunction to "offer the gift that Moses commanded"? But I refrain from pressing this difficulty. Enough has been said to explain why it is that, on the approach of sound criticism, the orthodox landmarks, which but lately seemed so steadfast, are one by one being removed: just as oftentimes, when air and light are admitted into the abode of the dead, the form which had been, and at first sight appeared still destined to be, long preserved, crumbles speedily away.

A Greek sage once laid down three rather sweeping propositions. (1) Nothing exists. (2) If anything exists, it may not be known. (3) If anything exists and may be known, the knowledge may not be communicated. Now, if in these propositions for "thing" be substituted "good argument against orthodoxy," they will be found to correspond to three objections commonly urged against inquiries like the present. With the first class of objectors—those who deny the existence of plausible arguments for rationalism—we have already dealt. There remain the other two sets of objectors. There are those who maintain that such plausible arguments exist indeed, but exist only to try our faith; the fruit of this tree of knowledge should be eschewed on pain of death. And there are those who complain that, in imparting to them this fruit, we have made them unhappy, and have driven them, as it were, out of Paradise: we have taken away their Lord, and they know not where we have laid him. This last objection shall be discussed first, and very briefly. That the popular creed is in itself not a happy one, we have shown. Indeed, the application of the name "Gospel" to a system containing such doctrines as the imputation of Adam's guilt—"th' enormous faith of many" damned "for one"—may be called the πρῶτον ψεῦδος of orthodoxy; insomuch that it is the Christian Universalists who are on *the side of the angels;* and this time it is the popular theology which, in representing itself as having received from the angels the glaring misnomer of "good tidings of great joy," suggests what is "little short of blasphemous." Still, although that theology is in itself a very Kakangel, there is no doubt that by many the κακάγγελτος ἄχη is unfelt. Our "sister while she prays" is generally able to enjoy "her early heaven, her happy views," and blissfully to ignore her early hell and most depressing views. And this is a reason against heedlessly airing modern opinions in general conversation, when one's hearer is almost at one's mercy. But it is not a reason against putting forth those opinions in writings, which no one is compelled to read. Moreover, the orthodox, who practise self-deception as to the unsound portions of their creed, will find their task daily more difficult, and therefore more demoralising. As we said in a former article, " the bracing intellectual air that we now breathe will bring the latent diseases of our religion out "; and perchance, if we limit overmuch the action of that bracing air, it will work unmixed harm—it will have time to bring the diseases out, but not time to cure them. It is on this account that too mild a treatment of those diseases may be perilous to the entire body of Christian sentiment and practice—not merely to the letter that killeth, but to the spirit that giveth life : if thine hand or thy foot offend thee, says the Scripture, cut it off. And thus, when we exhorted Christians manfully to renounce the devil and all his angels, and to drop hell out of the Bible, we acted under a Conservative impulse: for we doubted whether to Christianity itself the presence of those nether flames, if they were suffered to go on smouldering, would be wholly free from risk. *Behold, how great a matter a little fire kindleth.*

The other objection is, in effect, that "man is not made to question, but adore": it is *safer* to accept undoubtingly whatever our Bible or Church tells us of God, even if the evidence for those statements be inconclusive; nay, had the evidence been conclusive, where would be the room for our faith? Of this faith unfaithful we might summarily dispose, by observing that its possessors are liable to Coleridge's censure—they prefer Christianity to truth. They might, in a word, be designated by saying that *Malunt errare cum Christo quam nobiscum vera sentire.* And they might be encountered with the reverent, yet conclusive, answer, *Amicus Christus, magis amica veritas.* But it will serve our purpose to meet these objectors on their own ground, and to fight them with their own weapons. Is it, then, quite certain that a good Being, who on one or more occasions affirmed himself to have ordained Tophet, would wish his affirmation to be always believed? The answer to this question may be sought in human analogies. Malcolm in order to test the fidelity of Macduff, charged himself with grievous faults. It was with hearty satisfaction that Macduff at length discovered that Malcolm had been deceiving him. Nor can we doubt that, when the discovery was made, his satisfaction was shared by Malcolm himself; for the latter would prefer that his friend should regard him as an occasional liar, rather than as a perpetual villain.* A yet closer parallel may be drawn from classical mythology. Mr. Symonds has well observed that an enlightened Pagan would feel about the cannibal repasts attributed to his gods, much as an enlightened Christian feels about eternal punishment. This parallel (Mr. Symonds's critics notwithstanding) holds perfectly; for the analogical device which is used to defend, and the allegorical device which is used to explain away, the belief in a divine torture-house, may just as

* Perhaps a similar lesson may be gathered from the Gospels. We may be sure that the father whose son refused to go into the vineyard, but afterwards repented and went, was better pleased than if the son had kept his word and not gone—had been more truthful, but less obedient. The moral of Jephthah's story is less satisfactory; and the frantic efforts that are now-a-days made to explain away this simple narrative—to make believe that Jephthah broke his vow and did not commit murder—are among the many proofs that the religious instinct of modern times is in some respects healthier than that of the Old, and seemingly of the New, Testament. (Heb. xi. 32.)

readily be applied to the belief in divine cannibalism. It is, therefore, worth while to consider the sort of language which devout but enlightened Pagans—Pagan Broad Churchmen, in fact—held concerning this unsavoury dogma of Pagan orthodoxy. In a passage translated and justly praised by Bacon, Plutarch observes : " Surely, I had rather a great deal men should say, there was no such man at all as Plutarch, than that they should say that there was one Plutarch that would eat his children as soon as they were born; as the poets speak of Saturn;" the gods, he infers, have a similar preference, and hate superstition worse than Atheism. This principle is fruitful of consequences. Let us suppose that Plutarch would have accepted them: in that case, if Kronos or Zeus could have been shown to have pleaded guilty to revolting cruelty, Plutarch would have judged it right to disbelieve the Divine confession. And he might fairly have hoped that such a judgment would find an echo amid the peaks of Olympus; for, would not the Olympian father more bitterly resent the charge of murdering his own children, than that of, humanly speaking, either deceiving, or being deceived ($\kappa\rho\epsilon\hat{\iota}\tau\tau o\nu\ \delta'\hat{\epsilon}\lambda\acute{\iota}\sigma\theta\alpha\iota\ \psi\epsilon\hat{\upsilon}\delta o\varsigma\ \hat{\eta}\ \dot{\alpha}\lambda\eta\theta\grave{\epsilon}\varsigma\ \kappa\alpha\kappa\acute{o}\nu$)? Nay, further, Zeus was the father " of men " as well as " of gods," the father " whose offspring we are";* and the foregoing argument would as clearly apply to his treatment of his human, as to his treatment of his divine, children. Wherefore Plutarch might have thought it, not merely unscientific, but irreligious, to doubt that,

> "As for the dog, the furies, and their snakes,
> The gloomy caverns and the burning lakes,
> And all the vain infernal trumpery,
> They neither are, nor were, nor e'er can be."†

In other words, he might have clung to his belief in the divine mercy, even though the divine mercy had to be upheld at the cost of lesser divine attributes; even though, with the voracity of Tartarus, he gave up the veracity of Zeus.

Another Neopagan has dealt with divine cannibalism in a manner whereon Neochristians would do well to meditate. To Pindar it seemed hardly credible that the gods should have eaten up Pelops. He granted, indeed, that very strange things sometimes happened; and he thought that, in this particular case, the final

---

* See Acts xvii. 28. Epictetus says,—" If a man could fully realise this doctrine, that we are all in a special manner born of God, and that God is the father, both of men and of gods, I suppose that he would never have any ignoble or mean thoughts about himself. If Cæsar adopted you, your arrogance would be insufferable; and, when you know that you are the son of Zeus, will you not be elated?"

† Lucretius, translated by Dryden.

decision might be reserved for posterity; but, provisionally, he deemed it safer to reject the story.* It is remarkable that here the poet uses the same sort of prudential weapon that orthodox Christians use; but he uses it on the opposite side—he employs it in defence, not of faith, but of scepticism. And this should show us what a two-edged weapon it is. Pindar, indeed, probably regarded the gods as having been misrepresented, not as misrepresenting themselves. But we have shown that, for practical purposes, these two forms of misrepresentation differ less than at first sight appears; and, indeed, that the distinction between gods who misreport themselves, and gods who are misreported by verbally inspired reporters, is a distinction without a difference. But Pindar haply did not regard the misreporters as verbally inspired.† If so, his view exactly

---

* ἀμέραι δ'ἐπίλοιποι
μάρτυρες σοφώτατοι.
ἔστι δ'ἀνδρὶ φάμεν ἐοικὸς ἀμφὶ δαιμόνων καλά. μείων γὰρ αἰτία.

† Yet both Homer and Hesiod (ἐνέπνευσαν δὲ μοι αὐδὴν θείαν ἵνα κλείοιμι τά τ'ἐσσόμενα πρό τ' ἐόντα) claimed what would now be called verbal inspiration; so that Neopaganism may have had the same sort of difficulty in attributing to them any inspiration short of verbal, that Neochristianity has in attributing such partial inspiration to the Bible. It may be worth mentioning that Plutarch expressed his belief in the partial inspiration of oracles; the prophecies came from God—the bad Greek from the Pythoness.

foreshadowed that of the Neochristians: and the state of mind common to both bears so closely on our inquiry that we propose to consider it further, and for that purpose to resort, yet once again, to a classical illustration. The Kymæans being commanded by an oracle to deliver up a suppliant, one of their citizens, Aristodikus, suspected that the divine words had been tampered with,* and consulted the oracle himself. The god, however, gave the same answer as before. Thereupon Aristodikus bethought him of a device: he robbed the nests of the sacred birds that were in the precincts of the temple. Presently he heard a voice from the sanctuary, saying, "Wretch, how dare you strip the temple of my suppliants?" "O King," replied he, nothing abashed, "you indeed protect your suppliants; and do you bid the Kymæans deliver up theirs?"† "Yea, verily," said the god, "that for such impiety ye may perish speedily; and may never again ask the oracle about giving up suppliants." Thus, then, was Aristodikus rewarded for disregarding

* Δοκέων τοὺς θεοπρόπους οὐ λέγειν ἀληθέως. Hdt. i. 158.
† These words are closely parallel to passages in the Gospel: Matt. vi. 14, 15.; xviii. 33. Observe that, in all such passages, the identity of the divine and the human morality is assumed.

an injunction strikingly analogous to Jehovah's "statutes that were not good." His bearing in face of such an injunction differed from that of Abraham and Hosea,* just as Hellenism differed from Hebraism. It is therefore important that his precise moral attitude should be noted. He first cherished the hope that the wicked command was not from God; and afterwards, when convinced that it *was* from God, he still held that God was less dishonoured by its breach than by its observance; for it seemed less incredible that, for some inscrutable reason, God should have deceived his worshippers, than that he should have sanctioned what was unjust and cruel.

Aristodikus, in so judging, was a model of pious discrimination. He deserves our respect both for regarding the divine untruthfulness as one of the solutions of the problem that lay before him, and also for regarding it as an unsatisfactory solution—a solution not to be adopted till a happier one had failed. And, in thus expressing our concurrence with his estimate of divine deceptions, we have shown what we think of Mr. Oxenham's estimate. It is in a certain sense true that the belief in such deceptions is "little short of blasphemous." But this is a one-sided truth, unless supplemented by the more obvious and

* Gen. xxii. Hosea i.

momentous truth, that the belief in hell is, in the words of the first of living bishops, "blasphemous and revolting." Orthodoxy, therefore, is in a strait betwixt two blasphemies; and of those blasphemies she should choose the less.

Briefly, then, we concede to Suarez and Professor Huxley* that "Incredibile est, Deum illis verbis ad populum fuisse locutum quibus deciperetur." But we guard this concession by adding, "Incredibilius est, Deum illis paenis in populum esse usurum quibus crucietur." We should hate, not the belief in divine untruthfulness less, but the belief in divine cruelty more. Only, in holding our brief for Neochristianity, we assumed that it was between these two beliefs that the alternative lay. And, starting with this assumption, we maintained that those who *hang* the belief in hell on the divine veracity, represent the chain of evidence for hell as stronger than its weakest link; or, to employ a yet bolder metaphor, they make the burning lake rise above its own level. To prove this has been the design of our article. We have been endeavouring to show the universal application of a plain rule of human jurisprudence, by establishing a proposition which may be called a counterpart, if not a corollary, of Hume's famous proposition about miracles.

* "Mr. Darwin and his Critics."

Our proposition is: That no Person (whether in heaven or on earth) should stand convicted, on his own testimony, of an immoral or unlikely act, unless it be less antecedently unlikely that he should do the act than that his testimony should be false; "and" (to apply Hume's very words) "even in that case there is a mutual destruction of arguments, and the superior only gives us an assurance suitable to that degree of force which remains after deducting the inferior."

NOTE.

Since writing the article, I have had several proofs that the divinity and the fallibility of Christ *are* sometimes held together.* For instance: Robertson, in his sermon on "The Last Utterances of Christ," thus comments on the words, "Why hast thou forsaken me?":—"It is plain from this expression that the Son of God *felt* as if He had been deserted by his Father. We know that He was not deserted by Him. . . . And they who maintain that this was real desertion, attribute that to the Lord of Love which can alone belong to Judas—the desertion of innocence,—therefore we conclude that it arose from the infirmities of our Master's innocent human nature. It was the darkening of his human soul, not the hiding of God's countenance. He was worn, faint, and exhausted; his body was hanging from four lacerated wounds; and, more than that, there was much to perplex the Redeemer's human feelings, for He was suffering there, the innocent for the guilty." One may fairly ask: If the Redeemer, in the very act of redeeming, was "per-

* See "Safe Studies," page 376.

plexed" by the theory of redemption—nay, if He could at that awful moment attribute to his Father conduct which can alone belong to Judas—when, and on what, was He infallible?

I am assured that Lectures (answering more or less to the Bampton Lectures) have lately been delivered in Scotland, starting from the Christian standpoint, and advocating opinions not unlike those of the foregoing article. They are called *Kenosis*, from Phil. ii. 7, where it is said that Christ "made himself of no reputation," or (more literally) "emptied himself." These words might be taken as the text of my article, which is designed to show that the kenosis involved in the Incarnation may be a complete one, inasmuch as, even from the orthodox point of view, the doctrine itself is beset with seeming contradictions.

" Quid enim diversius esse putandum est
Aut magis inter se disjunctum discrepitansque,
Quam mortale quod est immortali atque perenni?"

In a word, Divinity unalloyed with Humanity implies Omniscience as well as Infallibility: if, in becoming Man, Christ *pro tempore* emptied himself of Omniscience (Mark xiii. 32), may He not also have emptied himself of Infallibility?

APPENDIX I.

RECOLLECTIONS OF PATTISON.

(Reprinted from the "Journal of Education" of June, 1885.)

RECOLLECTIONS OF PATTISON.

" Spectateur dans l'univers, le penseur sait que le monde ne lui appartient que comme sujet d'étude, et que le rôle de réformateur suppose presque toujours en ceux qui se le donnent des défauts et des qualités qu'il n'a pas."—RENAN.

IT was at Biarritz, in March, 1882, that I made Pattison's acquaintance.* I saw much of him then, and again, six months later, when he came to join me in Switzerland. In June, 1883, we met for the last time. He took most kindly to me from the first, and in our conversations he spoke with an absence of reserve which I understand to have been unusual with him. It will, however, be seen that my personal intercourse with him was confined to a short period. I have been fortunate in obtaining the help of several of his oldest friends, who have enabled me to make my portrait of him less imperfect. In the following sketch I propose to discuss fully one aspect of his character, which seems to me to be misunderstood; in other matters, I shall as far as

* Mr. Althaus, in his very interesting and appreciative Essay on Pattison, refers to this visit, and to the philosophical dialogues of which Biarritz was the scene.

possible restrict myself to a record of some of his opinions and characteristic sayings, so as to let him be his own interpreter.

One more personal detail by way of preface. The Rector took an unmerited interest in my Essays (contributed chiefly to the *Fortnightly Review*); and he insisted that I should publish them in a collected form, or else print them for private circulation, or at any rate that I should inform him of the names and dates of the articles, so that he might procure copies. For private reasons I chose the second alternative: my two volumes, *Safe Studies* and *Stones of Stumbling*, are at present unpublished; but copies of them (besides being thrown broadcast among friends) have been presented to the chief public libraries,* and are thus made accessible to readers. I am obliged to mention these facts, since a few of the Rector's sayings, which will be quoted, relate to passages in those volumes.

Wishing to learn the present state of Oxford, I observed to Pattison that in my time (1856-60) most of the able undergraduates were strong

* As two friendly reviewers of my volumes have urged me to publish them, I should like to mention that they have been presented to the British Museum, the Bodleian, the Cambridge University, the Oxford and Cambridge Unions, the three University Clubs in London, the Athenæum, the Savile and Albemarle Clubs, the Royal Institution, and the London Library Copies will be sent to any public library, on application to the publisher of the *Journal of Education*.

Liberals, both in politics and in theology, and I asked whether the same could be said of the present generation of undergraduates. In reply, he told me, doubtless with some exaggeration, that the opinions of the undergraduates are in chronic opposition to those of their tutors. It takes about twenty years for a budding student to grow into a full-blown don. Whence it follows that there are cycles of about forty years, during half of which the University rises in Liberalism, while during the other half it falls; or rather, the dons and the undergraduates are at the opposite ends of an intellectual seesaw, so that while the former are rising the latter are falling, and *vice versâ*. "When you were at Oxford," he said to me, "all the good men were Liberals; *they couldn't help it*. But now it is all changed. Many of the able undergraduates are Conservative; and those of an original turn take up Æstheticism"!

One who was his pupil in 1850 writes :—

" In my own case, the greatest piece of intellectual insight he showed was in persuading me to give up Natural Science as my main pursuit. 'You care for the literature of science, and for the results of science; you don't really care for science itself. You read Bacon and Herschel's *Introduction*, and the *Vestiges*, and Humboldt's *Cosmos;* but you don't come into chapel with the mud of Shotover and the railway cuttings sticking to your knees.'"

The same pupil told Pattison, rather apologetically, that, having been brought up in Scotland, he had never learnt the Greek Grammar, but had only used it as a book of reference. "I am delighted to hear it," was the unexpected reply; "far too much time is wasted on the Greek grammar." This view of Pattison's was all the more remarkable, because it was expressed thirty-five years ago.

I learn from the same source that Pattison (then sub-Rector) said to some of his most hardworking pupils, "I will let you off my lectures on Thursdays, on condition that you promise to make the day a complete holiday." He evidently thought that more intellectual good, or less physical harm, would follow from hard work for (say) six hours a day for five days in the week, than from hard work for five hours a day for six days.

A more recent pupil, intending to write for a Prize Essay, was urged by the Rector to begin at once: "No amount of hurried reading at the end will take the place of the process of slow gestation." Pattison might have said (employing Mr. Galton's metaphor) that a writer's thoughts ought to be long kept within call in "the antechamber of consciousness," before they are summoned to the presence chamber. The principle involved in the above advice was a favourite one with him. He always insisted that any one engaged in literary work ought, for the time being, to give up all practical avocations. He, of course, did not forget that Bacon, Macaulay, and countless others attained great literary success amid the distractions of public life; but he would probably have contended that those giants, had they been able to devote themselves exclusively to literature, might have attained a yet greater success, and that ordinary mortals, if they do not so devote themselves, will attain no success at all.

Certainly his standard of the requirements of a literary life was rigid to the verge of pedantry. A very able (and far too penitent) friend of his writes:

"He suggested that I should edit Selden's *Table Talk*. The preparation was to be, first to get the contents practically by heart, then to read the whole printed literature of Selden's day, and of the generation before him. In twenty years he promised me that I should be prepared for the work. He put the thing before me in so unattractive a way that I never did it or anything else worth doing. I consider the ruin of my misspent life very largely due to that conversation."

That this severe judgment on the Rector may not be taken too literally, I will quote from the same letter, "He was one of the best friends I ever had. He was not in the least donnish when one came to know him."

One learns without surprise that, in the words of a near relation, "he had a quite human fondness for his books; nothing annoyed him so much as to hear one of them fall; and dusting them, which he reduced to a science, seemed to give him real pleasure. In his last illness the sight of any of his favourites depressed him greatly. 'Ah!' he would say, 'I am to leave my books,' and sometimes, 'They have been more to me than my friends.' He would ask for them one after the other, till he was literally covered almost to his shoulders as he lay, and the floor around him was strewn with them. He used to say that the sight of books was necessary to him at his work; and, once reading how Schiller always kept 'rotten apples' in his study because their scent was beneficial to him, he pointed to some shelves above his head, where he kept his oldest and most prized editions, and said: 'There are my rotten apples.'"

Such severe comments are often passed on clergymen who accept the dogmas of their church in a spiritual, not a literal, sense, that I feel some scruple in recording Pattison's comments on the orthodox theology. But one circumstance reassures me. Some of us can remember only too well the consternation with which, thirteen years ago, members of London Society learnt that one of their own body, the Duke of Somerset, was in the enemy's camp, and with what refreshing ease they let themselves be convinced that Archbishop

Thomson had put the Sadducees to silence. No one at all familiar with the Rector's later writings can doubt that his judgment on this controversy might have been conveyed in Henry VI.'s words:—

"I more incline to Somerset than York."

As Pattison himself has spoken so plainly,* I need not mind speaking plainly also. Nevertheless, "Haud ignota loquor" is not my only apology for publishing what he said to me; I have obtained an assurance from those authorized to speak on his behalf that they in no wise object to the publication.

I asked him how it was that, being so very outspoken in his writings, he yet seemed never to burn his fingers, as other Broad Church clergymen did. He answered that, as a matter of fact, he had burnt his fingers, but that he would have burnt them much worse if the outspoken passages had occurred in theological writings: editors entrusted such books as the *Life of Milton* to the

---

* I have elsewhere (*Stones of Stumbling*, p. 46) quoted Grote's opinion that the success of Christianity was one of the greatest calamities that ever befell the human race. Did he mean much more by this than Pattison (Memoirs, p. 96) meant by saying that "the triumph of the Church organization over the wisdom and philosophy of the Hellenic world .... is, to the Humanist, the saddest moment in history— the ruin of the painfully constructed fabric of civilization to the profit of the Church"?

tender mercies of lay critics—such books as Mr. Jowett's Commentary on St. Paul to the untender mercies of clerical ones. He told me that at one period he had been on the point of turning Catholic, and that he had been deterred chiefly by observing that on political and scientific questions—the only questions which admit of being directly tested—the Catholic Church had been time after time in the wrong. He admitted that he had become much more Liberal even than he was when he sent his contribution to *Essays and Reviews*.

He was asked whether he did not think that the attempts made by Archdeacon Farrar and others to show that the eternity of punishment cannot be demonstrated from the Gospels, are utterly futile. He expressed his assent by saying, "If they can explain away the word αἰώνιος, there are perfectly clear expressions to the same effect in other texts." He was therefore of opinion that the belief in the non-eternity of punishment involves the postulate that the Master's words, as reported in the Gospels, contain errors. I had adopted the same view in an article in the *Fortnightly Review* (December, 1877). I begged him to read the article carefully through, and to tell me whether it contained anything to which rational objection could be taken. After reading it over, he found only one trifling matter to which he at all demurred.*

He used the term "economy" (that is, husbanding, *ménagement*) "of truth" to denote the practice of answering fools according to their folly, and of speaking parables to them that are without. I was so struck with the phrase that, in reprinting my article, mentioned in the last paragraph, I rechristened it "Divine Economy of Truth"; but I first wrote to ask the Rector what authority there was for the phrase which he so often employed. He answered:—

"I almost think a tract of Keble in *Tracts for the Times* was the first in our day to bring up the word 'Economy' in the sense you mean. But this was a revival, not an original invention. The Greek fathers not seldom speak of the οἰκονομίας σωτηρίου—as we say, the Christian 'dispensation.' The idea is, that revelation itself is only a veil, half revealing, half concealing, and so a test or touchstone of earnest minds, only such being willing to wait and learn. And, as God

---

* He thought that perhaps I made too much of Jer. vii. 22 (*Stones of Stumbling*, p. 102). I was glad to be informed by so comparatively orthodox a divine as Dr. Baldwin Brown that he had read my article with sympathy, and that he thought that the next step taken by the Broad Church party will perhaps be to impugn the infallibility of the words reported in the Gospels. Tillotson suggests, in Sermon xxxv., that God may have represented future punishment as more horrible than it really is to be, the exaggeration being the only possible way of deterring men from sin. Compare Selden's *Table Talk*, s.v. *Damnation*.

dispenses crumbs of truth to the chosen, so in the visible Church the clergy are dispensers to their flock of so much truth as they think good for them. Keble's tract is entitled, 'On reserve in communicating religious knowledge.' 'God punishes with mental blindness those who approach religious questions with a speculative mind' is his dictum—the text about casting pearls before swine is dwelt upon."

A Catholic nobleman, who lived near Holywell, once gave me an extraordinary account of a man, to all appearance blind for many years, who recovered his sight after resorting to that sacred spring. On my mentioning this incident, Pattison said, "It is seldom possible to sift the evidence in such cases. There is only one real test. Give the Holywell water to the inmates of a blind-asylum, and see whether it cures them." A Catholic would, of course, object that the application of such a test would imply want of faith, and that God would punish this want of faith by refusing to work the miracle.* Pattison would have declared, and I certainly should not deny, that this objection is irrational. I merely insist that, in pronouncing it to be irrational, we are claiming the right of transferring, not this question only, but every similar one, from the Theo-

* Orthodox Protestants made a similar objection to Sir Henry Thompson's proposed method of testing the objective efficacy of prayer. I would commend to their notice two *experimenta fidei* sanctioned in the Bible: Judges vi. 36—40; 1 Kings xviii. 23—39.

logical to the Scientific Court of Appeal; we are making the assumption that a knowledge of natural laws is our mainstay, just as reliance on supernatural aid was the mainstay of our fathers —in a word, that "our valours are our best gods," and that Prudence is Providence writ small.

The Rector's attention was called to the startling amount of evidence which Herodotus brings forward on behalf of portents which we now reject as a matter of course; and he was asked whether, after pondering on that evidence, he did not doubt the conclusiveness of the testimony, even of the "500 brethren at once," which is adduced by a more famous writer in support of a far greater miracle. "What weight," asked he, "can you attach to such testimony? It rests on the *ipse dixit* of a single reporter, who places his own vision on the same level with the rest of the evidence." In reference to the prophetic, I mean *predictive,* power which is claimed for the Founders of Christianity, he made the remark: Of all the momentous events that have occurred since the destruction of Jerusalem, not one was foretold in the New Testament. He defined orthodoxy as "Stoicism *plus* a legend."

It will be convenient to speak of his political forebodings further on. At present I will merely mention that he considered political pessimism to be on the increase, and that he attributed the increase to two causes. The first cause is, the disappointment which was felt by Liberals after 1848. He exclaimed with exaggerative vehemence: "Before 1848 men expected to get everything by revolutions; they soon learnt that they were not a bit better off than before." The second cause is an indirect and negative one. Men are apt to infer from the Divine Goodness that good *must* be the final goal of ill, and that an increasing purpose *must* run through all the ages. And, as a matter of fact, men commonly hold that the nineteenth century fares (so to say) better than the eighteenth, and the eighteenth than the seventeenth; therefore, the twentieth will fare better than the nineteenth, and for evermore each $n+1^{th}$ will fare better than each nth. But, alas, this vision of an earthly Paradise men of science are ruthlessly consigning to dreamland. Either freezing or frying, they tell us, is to be the lot of our remote descendants; and this unpleasing catastrophe is likely to be ushered in by long ages of decline: during those ages each $n+1^{th}$ century will fare *worse* than each nth. Of course, this does not prove that the twentieth will fare worse than the nineteenth. But it breaks the spell of the à *priori* reasoning on which, according to Pattison, the belief in progress mainly rests; and thus it infuses into philosophers a restless unfaith—a sentiment akin to that of δῖνος βασιλεύει τὸν Δί' ἐξεληλακώς, or at least to that of

> Usque adeo res humanas vis abdita quædam
> Obterit.

A few of the Rector's literary criticisms may find a place here. Some interest may be felt in the miscellaneous intellectual diet which he prescribed to me in a letter (14th October, 1883) :—

> "You will read Spielhagen's *Quisisana*, and Trollope's *Autobiography*. I myself find much fireside sympathy in Twining's *Reminiscences*—but it is mild tobacco, and has a special flavour of eighteenth century about it, which may not be to everyone's taste. Have you ever read A. Gellius' *Noctes Atticæ*? You will find some curious matters there, though perhaps Jevons' *Social Essays* may be more to your liking. Above all, read the speeches of the clericals at the Reading Congress—quite time for some one to rap them on the head."

He also urged me, and many other friends, to read Amiel's *Journal Intime*. May not his relish for Amiel's moral self-dissection have been due to his sympathy with one who suffered from great mental depression—depression aggravated by considering how much had been expected from him, and how little he had performed?[*]

To a friend who complained of not caring for the character of Æneas, Pattison observed that the interest of the Æneid is derived neither from

[*] See the *Note* at the end of this essay.

its characters nor from its plot, but merely from its being a Handbook of Roman Antiquities. This conversation probably occurred some years before he spoke to me on the same subject in very different terms. I understood him to say that the charm of Virgil lies in his power of exciting "successive waves of emotion" in the reader's mind. He read with very great interest Mr. Myers's Essay on the poet, which he described as something quite out of the common. He went the length of saying that, in the beauty of occasional passages, Virgil is unsurpassed by any poet, ancient or modern; and he gave as an instance the encomium on Italy (*Georg.* II. 136—176), which reaches its climax in the line,

"Salve, magna parens frugum, Saturnia tellus,
Magna virum."

He told me that he thought he should never like Dante, and he knew he should never like Carlyle. His aversion to Carlyle is referred to in a letter which I received from a member of his family:—

"I don't think that he cared at all about Carlyle; he used to call him a juggler with words, and to speak contemptuously of anything infected with his style. He belonged to the Browning Society, and even took the chair at one of its meetings, but he would not allow that Mr. Browning is a poet; he never read his works for pleasure, but merely to see what it was that people talked about. Wordsworth seemed to give him more pleasure than any English poet, and he loved to read Schiller's *Gedichte*. He was glad of an excuse for turning up Pope, and, if we met with a quotation from him in our reading, he would insist on finding the context, and reading it aloud with a peculiar swing and tone of voice which he always used for Pope. His delight over his favourite epigrams was most amusing. The couplet—

'On her white breast a sparkling cross she wore,
Which Jews might kiss, and infidels adore.'

he was never tired of declaring to be inimitable."

He told me that, in order to enjoy Wordsworth thoroughly, I ought to be familiar with the Lake district. Indeed, he seems to have thought it extremely important to take poets (in this literal sense) on their own ground. Miss Swanwick has kindly authorized me to mention that she was somewhat amused by the persistence with which he urged her to go all the way to Sicily in order to be able to appreciate Theocritus, "an acquaintance with Sicilian scenery, and with the Sicilian people, being, in his opinion, essential for the full enjoyment of the *Idylls*." She also informs me that, on their first meeting, he opened fire by asking, "Which do you think the finest poem in the world?" She replied that the question needed deliberation, and asked which *he* thought the finest poem. He at once answered, "The *Agamemnon*." She suggested that in such a comparison, other things being equal, the length of a poem must count for something, and that, therefore, the *Iliad* might have a prior claim. He, however, stuck to his opinion that the *Agamemnon* is "the grandest work of creative genius in the whole range of literature," and added that, the oftener he read it, the more he admired it.

Others of his friends besides Miss Swanwick had experience of his attempts to break the social ice by plunging headlong into a discussion. A very shy young lady, paying him a first visit, was startled by the question : " Which is your favourite English sonnet ? " He himself was especially fond of Wordsworth's sonnet on *Westminster Bridge*, and of Blanco White's only sonnet. I am told that he sometimes asked ladies what they thought of this last sonnet, as a sure test of their literary judgment. He cared little for *John Inglesant*. To a lady who inquired whether he liked it, he gave what in the *Art of Pluck* is called the *answer indirect:* " You are asking me what everybody asks me everywhere." I am now bordering on a province of my subject which I enter with some trepidation.

" Like all good men," says Mr. Leslie Stephen, " [Samuel] Johnson loved good women, and liked to have on hand a flirtation or two, as warm as might be within the bounds of due decorum." It is undeniable that this somewhat exclusive test of goodness would not exclude Pattison, who at times seemed to agree with the hero of *Amours de Voyage*, that *Vir sum, nihil fœminei a me alienum puto*. To speak more seriously, he sought and obtained what has been called the one compensation of growing old. The praise which Wordsworth bestowed on Nature, may more truly be applied to a good woman—she never yet betrayed the heart that loved her; and Pattison stood in special need of that restful sympathy which women know how to give, which good women will give when they feel that it is valued, but which men can neither give nor take away. Yet he learnt by experience that even this rose is not thornless. In particular, he found that the art of instructing and correcting women without affronting them is not easily acquired. The mode of its acquisition, like everything else in which he took an interest, he subjected to critical analysis. "The art of pleasing," I heard him say, "consists in entire self-effacement." This opinion is sanctioned by the high authority of Rochefoucauld (*Maximes*, 139); yet, for all that, it represents only a half-truth. Those who are always taking their own line — whose individuality asserts itself in their own despite — often make the deepest impression on the world. This quality is noticed by Goethe as the chief characteristic of Englishmen:—

"Their deportment in society is as full of confidence, and as easy as if they were lords everywhere and the whole world belonged to them. This it is which pleases our women.... They [Englishmen] have the courage to be that for which nature made them. There is nothing vitiated or spoilt about them, there is nothing half-way or crooked; but, such as they are, they are complete men. That they are also sometimes complete fools, I allow with all my heart; but that is still something, and has still always some weight in the scale of nature."*

The Rector, however, might fairly have rejoined that, now at any rate, the ordinary John Bull is not a favourite with Germans, and that a few lessons in self-effacement would do him no harm.

I drew Pattison's attention to a statement which he had made in an article in the *Academy*, that " it is difficult to be loved too much by one sex and enough by the other"; and I asked how he explained the anomaly. He answered that it is not so much that a lady's man (in the best sense of the term) excites jealousy in other men, but rather that there is something in his temperament by which they are repelled. May not the fact be that all women, except the very best, like " more self-effacement" in men, than men like in each other? Goethe has noted how hard and important it is in friendship to avoid being either too confidential or

* Eckermann's *Conversations* (Oxenford's translation). Compare Sterne's *Sentimental Journey*, *Character—Versailles*

too reserved. The difficulty is closely allied to one pointed out by Horace—to that of hitting the exact mean between *Scurrantis species* and *Asperitas agrestis et inconcinna*, the mean between being hypocritical and hypercritical, or rather between an excessive desire to please and a bluntness which degenerates into brutality. Unfortunately, women, as a rule, like the mean to incline towards the former of these extremes, while men like it to incline towards the latter. In support of this view, I will remark that women are pleased by a man who keeps conversation going, whereas men prefer one who seldom speaks unless he has something to say.

The Rector once reminded me what a different thing it is to understand a subject and to be able to teach it. He said this with special reference to the difficulty of teaching women unofficially. The social superiority of their sex has, as he expressed it, " passé dans les mœurs." And this superiority is wont to clash with the instructor's superiority in age and in knowledge. Female pupils do not receive the moral tonic which is given to male pupils. If they are silly or obstinate, their teacher seldom contradicts them sharply, and never ridicules them. The anomaly of this relation was felt by Pattison all the more, because he had rather strong views as to the intellectual inferiority of the average woman to the average man. Indeed, his love of paradox led him to speak as if he imagined *Ens rationale* to be the definition, not of *Homo*, but of *Vir*. I asked him what he thought of the unchivalrous remark attributed to Disraeli, that all women require flattery: did the author of this remark merely use the word *flattery* as a satirical equivalent to *égards?* did he merely mean that women receive and expect, in compensation for their weakness, a deferential homage from men not wholly unlike that which a Prime Minister pays to a constitutional Sovereign? "What Disraeli calls flattery," replied Pattison, "I call economy of truth. I feel that, when I, an old man of seventy, am talking on intellectual subjects to a young girl of seventeen, she and I are on quite different planes of thought; and it is necessary to translate my ideas into her language. If she talks nonsense, I take refuge in flight. I always agree; but, when she thinks that her prejudices are quite secure, I slowly try to undermine them." (He emphasized the word *undermine* by moving his out-stretched hand diagonally downwards.) Of his tendency to self-caricature — of his seeming to take the inverted motto, *Video pejora proboque*, without adding, *Sed meliora sequor* — more will be said presently. I will now merely observe that such utterances of his as the above are to be taken *cum grano salis*, or rather *cum pleno salino*. The truth which probably underlies his exaggeration is that, in arguing with women (always excepting the very best), it is hard for men to maintain the same perfect frankness, or rather directness, which they maintain in arguing with each other. The Rector, so far from being a dissembler or even a *self-effacer*, was in reality somewhat over-frank. He was visited by a young lady who wrote well, but who in his opinion talked less well. He resolved to admonish her of this defect; but, instead of trying in any of the thousand-and-one possible ways to hint, while commending her writings, that more was now expected of her discourse—*laudando præcipere*, as Bacon would have said,—he embarrassed her by the blunt rebuke: " Your conversational utterances are feeble."

The following abridgment of an account which he gave of his meeting an American young lady at a foreign *table d'hôte*, reproduces his characteristic sayings almost, if not quite, *verbatim :* " She was only nineteen, but she knew everything. She told me the exact amount of affection which the Princess C. has for her future husband; and she gave me a full account of the divorce laws in all the States of America. She appealed to me sometimes; of course I agreed. At last, she asked whether I did not think she could write a book; and I told her that she was the most ignorant girl I ever met! But I took care to say so in such a way that she couldn't mind it." I doubt not that in this description the Rector was jocularly overstating both the parts which he acted—the part of *assentator* and the part of candid friend. Still, after making allowance for such exaggeration, I wonder whether in the latter character he was quite as agreeable to the young lady as he imagined.

I asked him whether he agreed with Sainte-Beuve in thinking that the advice contained in Lord Chesterfield's *Letters* was such as Horace might have given to his son, if he had had one. The only answer which I could get from him was, "Horace would have thought a son a great bore." Yet he regarded Chesterfield's *Letters* as a repertory of maxims which might be useful to the social tactician. Indeed, he himself (as we have seen) was theoretically an adept in *gynæcology*—the science of womankind. But I doubt his being equally successful in the practical application of that science. A lady once complained, "The Rector treats me like an intellectual machine." And I suspect that in general, when he had but just removed the scales from a female pupil's eyes, he was too apt to shed on her a dry (or rather an achromatic) light—thought uncoloured by feeling.

On the whole, I am less disposed to think that he was much liked by all, or by most women, than that he was very much liked by a few.

Biography is sometimes autobiography in disguise. The following extract from the *Life of Milton* is obviously founded—indeed, its author admitted that it is founded—more or less on personal experience :—

"Milton longed to be loved that he might love again. But he had to pay the penalty of all who believe in their own ideas, in that their ideas come between them and the persons that approach them, and constitute a mental barrier which can only be broken down by sympathy. And sympathy for ideas is hard to find, just in proportion as those ideas are profound, far reaching, the fruit of long study and meditation. Hence it was that Milton did not associate readily with his contemporaries, but was affable and instructive in conversation with young persons, and those who would approach him in the attitude of disciples."

More than once, when "disciples" were staying with the Rector, he and they together concocted a translation which was sent in for the Prize offered by the *Journal of Education*. I was startled when he told me that one of these joint productions obtained only a 4th Class. At first I conjectured that this was a practical illustration of the maxim Οὐκ ἀγαθὸν πολυκοιρανίη—a mishap, such as often befalls a plurality of generals in the waging of war or a plurality of cooks in the making of broth. But

I found that this explanation would not serve: the Rector assured me that he revised the translation so thoroughly as to make it virtually his own. I was therefore still more amazed when I heard from a sleeping partner, so to say, in the translators' firm, that one of their compositions fell as low as the 7th Class. But my surprise was lessened when my informant added that Pattison's translation was a very free one—so free, indeed, that, finding sentiments or metaphors in the original which were not to his liking, he took upon himself to be wise above that which was written, and to idealise instead of reproducing!*

This masterful mode of translating tallies well with his strong desire that his pupils and friends should always use the best phrases and forms of speech. He protested even against the common error of calling a *sarcastic* smile a *sardonic* one. He and I once talked over the old tradition—a tradition mentioned, I think, by a Scholiast on Homer—from which the word "sardonic" is said to have sprung. In very early times the natives of Sardinia were wont to eat such of their countrymen as were worn out by age. But, as manners grew milder, it was not thought seemly that a patriarch should be thus doomed without his own

---

* Pattison would doubtless have endorsed Moritz Haupt's paradox, "Translation is the death of understanding."

consent; and, in proof that his consent was freely given, he was himself chosen to bid the guests. Such, however, was the force of public opinion (opponents of euthanasia should make a note of this) that the veteran always issued the invitations to the supper where, in Hamlet's phraseology, he would not eat but be eaten. The courteous smile which beamed on the old gentleman's countenance as he was doing this last act of hospitality—ἑκὼν ἀέκοντί γε θυμῷ—is the prototype of all sardonic smiles. For the truth of this ghastly story the Rector would not vouch; but he insisted that the word "sardonic" should be used in the sense which the story indicates. In short, he wished his pupils to remember that a sardonic laugh is a laugh at one's own expense, and on the wrong side of one's mouth. From the following remarks, it will appear that he himself laughed sardonically at the world.

The passage chosen as motto for this article has been severely condemned by Mazzini, and to many it may appear cynical. But I have chosen it as putting into a clear light the point of view from which Pattison should be judged. He once remarked to me emphatically, "There has only been one Goethe." Yet, on another occasion, he protested against the attempts that are often made to exalt Goethe into a moral hero, and even described him as stamping morality under his feet. This censure is doubtless exaggerated, and indeed was probably not meant to be taken literally. Yet the Rector's judgment of Goethe, both on its favourable and on its unfavourable side, has much in common with the following extract from a famous writer:—

"Chaque ordre de grandeur a sa maîtrise à part et ne doit point être comparé à d'autres. Un philanthrope qui, ayant à juger Goethe, le mettrait en parallèle avec Vincent de Paule, se trouverait amené à ne voir dans le plus grand génie des temps modernes qu'un égoiste qui n'a rien fait pour le bonheur et l'amélioration morale de ses contemporains."*

I quote this passage because Pattison, as well as Goethe, has been accused of moral insensibility. The charge against the Rector is unjust, but not wholly inexplicable. He was, at least in his later years, essentially a scholar, valuing the spread of knowledge more

"Than aught, divine or holy, else enjoyed
In vision beatific."

The French employ their barely translatable term *l'idéal* to include *le vrai*, *le beau*, and *le bien*. It would seem that many persons who devote

---

* A similar sentiment is expressed by Mommsen when contrasting the merits of the Romans with those of the Greeks. The passage is quoted in *Safe Studies*, p. 278, Note.

themselves to seeking *l'idéal* through *le beau* or through *le vrai*, have a special difficulty in seeking it through what in the narrower sense may be called *le bien:* in other words, scholars and philosophers often lack the enthusiasm of humanity. This is one reason why saints and sages so seldom quite understand one another. Dean Church can as little do justice to Bacon as Bacon could have written the *Life of St. Anselm.*

In order to illustrate further our view of Pattison's ethical languor, it will be needful to dwell at some length on his scepticism and cynicism. He told me that he objected to auricular confession chiefly because it made people examine themselves too closely. He expressed this opinion in reply to a question as to what he thought of the following sentiment of Goethe:—

"It has at all times been said and repeated that man should strive to know himself. This is a singular requisition, with which no one complies, or indeed ever will comply. . . . I know not myself, and God forbid I should."

How was it that, whereas the greatest moral teacher of antiquity took as his motto, "Know thyself," this great modern teacher virtually said, "Know not thyself"? Are the two maxims as much opposed to one another as at first sight appears? The answer probably is that they are not; for, while Socrates addressed his exhortation to the mass of men, Goethe limited his admonition to the few who are possessed with the demon of self-consciousness. Our meaning will be made clearer by an illustration. Aurora Leigh says, of one whom she elsewhere calls a "good" man, that

> "He sets his virtues on so raised a shelf,
> To keep them at the grand millennial height,
> He has to mount a stool to get at them;
> And, meantime, lives on quite the common way,
> With everybody's morals."

Now, it is plain that, when this "good" man acquiesced (as almost everyone acquiesces) in the moral code of those around him, more qualms would be felt by him than by men whose ideal was less exalted; and also that, if he was given to honest introspection, those qualms might become very inconvenient. It is indeed possible that, by fostering this introspection, he would be converted into a hero. But it is quite as likely that he would be unfitted for action, would become powerless to prevent the pale cast of his thoughts from discolouring resolution and enthusiasm—$\varphi\iota\lambda o\sigma o\varphi\epsilon\hat{\iota}\nu$ ἄνευ μαλακίας. The fact seems to be that, while most good men require the brightest ideals of character and conduct to light them on the road to virtue, the too clear sight of some philosophers is dazzled by the contrast between the brightness of those ideals and the dark shade of the actual. Cynicism is, as it were, the smoked glass which these latter employ to prevent being dazzled overmuch.

We never, says Goethe, feel so much at ease with our own consciences as when we are dwelling complacently on the faults of others. And it is by reason of the restlessness of the intellectual conscience that the intellectual man of the world is tempted to use cynical language, which shocks and startles unintellectual men who are not a bit less worldly than himself.* We thus understand why Talleyrand, being informed of two faults of a lady of his acquaintance, exclaimed, " Elle est détestable, elle n'a que ces deux fautes-là "; why Disraeli, if rightly reported, censured a Liberal statesman as not having even " a redeeming vice"; why Goethe maintained that Spinozism, when manipulated by reflection, becomes Machiavellism; and why Gibbon seems happier when discovering the sins of the good and the follies of the wise, even than when relating the murder of a priest.

It is probable that one cause of the strange

* It is my experience that, while most intellectual *men* prefer Thackeray to Dickens, nearly all *women* prefer Dickens to Thackeray. If this is so, is it not because women, being rarely troubled with self-knowledge, have no relish for cynicism?

repugnance which such men as these feel for heroic virtue, is to be found in their sympathy with those whose welfare has been more or less directly, more or less completely, sacrificed—with the sons of Brutus and the brother of Timoleon. But a more important cause is, that a degree of disinterestedness, of which introspective minds are even too apt to think themselves incapable, is contemplated in others only with pain.

These considerations are meant to explain, not to justify, the ordinary type of cynicism. They must be pushed somewhat further to cover the case of Pattison. A distinguished pupil of his assures me that, at the time of the Tractarian movement, he had a high spiritual ideal, that he lost that ideal when he changed his views, and that he keenly felt the loss of it.* At this crisis of his life, he had much in common with the exiled Psalmist, whose affections would not take root in a strange country, and who looked wistfully back on the days when *Stantes erant pedes*

---

* This paragraph had been written before I had read the *Memoirs*; I leave it in its original form as an independent testimony. To Pattison may be applied some of Macaulay's remarks about Shrewsbury, who, after a long and painful struggle, shook off the yoke of his early Catholic training: "The shock which had overturned his early prejudices had at the same time unfixed all his opinions" [and some of his principles].—*History*, Vol. II., p. 128, ed. 1866.

nostri in atriis tuis, Jerusalem. To the typical scholar of our generation may be applied the words of its typical poet:—

> "Of all the creatures under heaven's wide cope,
> We are most hopeless, who had once most hope,
> And most beliefless, that had most believed."

It is not impossible that the line preceding these,

> "Eat, drink, or die, for we are souls bereaved,"

would express the despairing state into which he fell. A great writer has remarked that we feel what our ancestors thought, and that posterity will feel what we think. May not much of the spiritual anguish of our generation be due to the fact that many of us think with philosophers, while feeling with theologians? It was perhaps through being in this condition that Pattison continued long in the Slough of Despond. There is even reason to fear that, for some years, the loss of the ideal had on him a natural but melancholy effect, similar to that which (in the fable) the loss of the tail had on the fox. It is, however, right to mention that his mental struggles affected his nerves, and that these reacted on his mental condition. Speaking of his state at this time, my friend writes:

> "What his physical condition was then,—without being ill,—may be judged from one fact. He most kindly gave

me a private lecture in *Magna Charta;* we both adopted the position of seekers. During an animated discussion of Hallam's views, I turned aside to collate some reading. On looking round, Pattison was fast asleep; and this is how he often seemed in those years, wearied out with vexations, and as if he might sink into an exhausted sleep at any moment."

It should also be stated that my informant was intimate with Pattison chiefly when he was smarting under a sense of grievous injustice after the failure of his first candidature for the Rectorship; and it is thought that haply, for some years, the loss of his ideal and the loss of his election combined to give bitterness to his conversation. This is important as throwing light both on the origin and on the original form of his cynicism. But, when I knew him, his state of mind was different. I never detected in him the least resemblance to the *esprit fort* (or *faible*) who exclaimed: "Lord, I cannot believe; help thou mine unbelief." His cynicism seemed to me to be the outcome of deliberate reason, and to have become a second nature to him: and as such J shall attempt to describe it.

"It is not desirable," says Bagehot, "to take this world too much *au sérieux;* most persons will not; and the one in a thousand who will, should not." In other words, a man of that abnormal type ought to make a conscious effort, if not to become what the French call a *farceur,* and what Bacon in his essay on *Fortune* calls *poco di matto*, at least to avoid being righteous over-much, and being over-wise. This was just the sort of exhortation which Pattison needed, which he knew that he needed, and which he tried, not very successfully, to follow: he was, as it were, an *homme sérieux malgré lui*.

If I were asked to what he owed this peculiarity of temperament, I should say that it was partly due to his retentiveness of memory, or rather to his inability to forget. Darwin, in explaining the genesis of morals among primitive men, attributes much to the influence of memory. When the best of our early ancestors saw a neighbour suffering, they were haunted by the recollection of what they themselves had suffered. When they were tempted to do wrong, they could not always banish the thought of their own resentment when injured. This *importunateness* of memory, arising under different conditions and associated (as it often is) with nervous weakness, contributes much both to the merits and to the defects of such men as the Rector: they cannot get rid of their former selves. Of the many illustrations of my meaning, the most obvious must suffice. When a man labours to avert or to postpone a change which he regards as hurtful or premature, it is

M

hardly possible for him to avoid exaggerating the evils of that change, and thus becoming an alarmist. When another or the same man seeks to evolve the energy needful for carrying out some great reform or establishing a scientific truth, it is perhaps impossible for him to avoid greatly exaggerating the importance of his undertaking, and thus becoming a strong optimist. It is through this and other causes that nearly every one of us oscillates between a modified pessimism (or at least uneasiness about the future) and a decided optimism; and during these oscillations an ordinary Philistine, however strong his affirmations may be on either side, has an enviable faculty of believing in himself. To Pattison and his peers this convenient self-deception is impossible. Their Liberal zeal is checked by the unwelcome memory of their fits of pessimism, and their Conservative zeal by the memory of their fits of optimism. No doubt, they are thus preserved from much extravagance; but they tend, in the phraseology of Burns, to become "tideless blooded." This word exactly expresses Pattison's chief fault, or rather his *misfortune;* for it was his misfortune that states of feeling which appear to ordinary men as a series of dissolving views, each distinct in itself, blended themselves before his mind's-eye and made a sort of blur.* Renan has said, "Presque tous nous sommes doubles," and has somewhere maintained the paradox: "Woe to the man who does not contradict himself at least once a day."† In a like spirit, Pattison, when reminded that some principle or policy which he was upholding was opposed to principles laid down in his writings, used to exclaim jestingly, "It is more than five minutes ago that I wrote that," or again, "Who ever dreamt of reconciling practice and theory?" Yet, while thus professing indifference, he was really anxious, perhaps over-anxious, to see practice and theory fitting one another like hand and glove. To quote again from the writer who so well illustrates this subject: "The man," says Goethe, "who would do all that is expected of him, must overrate himself a little—perhaps more

---

* Since writing this, I have learnt that he once quoted the following passage (from Lewes's *Life of Goethe*) in explanation of his own character: "There is in men of active intellects, and especially in men of imaginative, apprehensive intellects, a fluctuation of motives keeping the volition in abeyance, which practically amounts to weakness. This is the weakness of imaginative men." This reminds one of Macaulay's character of Halifax.

† Mr. Maurice notes "one important quality of Boswell. He never stumbled at contradictions. Johnson often said things directly inconsistent with each other. Most thoughtful men who speak what they mean, and feel strongly at any given time, do."

than a little, if he thinks about himself at all." And, on the other hand, he who dwells constantly on the seamy side of his own work, needs to be reminded that there is just as seamy a side to the work of others, or he will think himself the worst sempster in the world. In the phrase of the eminent Oxonian who is now, as he was thirty years ago, the greatest teacher in the University, such a man is too much "under the dominion of logic." Pattison was under that dominion; and, when logical power, mnemonic power, and nervous weakness are combined as they were in him, they indicate a person to whom, not indeed *pecca fortiter*, but μάθε παίζειν would be wholesome advice:

> "amara lento
> Temperet risu; nihil est ab omni
> Parte beatum."

Such a man as we have described could hardly fail to be given to paradoxes; and, in fact, as we have already intimated, Pattison revelled in them. Sometimes he was paradoxically sceptical. I once asked him whether it is not certain that we owe much to the Catholic Church for the wisdom with which in the Middle Ages she insisted on the celibacy of the priests, as the only means of securing their independence of the barons. "We always say so," was his characteristic rejoinder, "but I don't know on what evidence." On one occasion, his paradoxical temper found vent in an anti-Liberal ebullition worthy of Carlyle:—"I should like to see the anniversary of the day on which Cromwell closed the door of the House of Commons kept as the greatest day of our calendar." This, however, seems to have represented a passing phase of his opinions; for I am assured that he sometimes defended constitutional government as the least unsatisfactory of all forms of government. I once discussed with him the singular superiority, in point of ability, of the Liberal to the Conservative party in the House of Commons. "Yes," he observed, "the best thing about parliamentary government is that it tends to bring the ablest men to the front."

I spoke to him about the last patriarch of Benthamism, Mr. George Norman, who, like his friend, Mr. Grote, inclined to Conservatism in his old age. Mr. Norman once said to me, "I only wish that Gladstone would leave us without organic changes for the next forty years" (a sentiment which sounds very like "Après moi *et mon fils* le déluge"): and, on another occasion, he made the gloomy prediction: "Sooner or later, there must be a struggle between *those who have got* and *those who want*, and I don't see how it is to be settled except by the sword. But I suppose that *those who have got* will win." "True," said Pattison, when this augury of ill was repeated to him; "in the end *those who have got* will win. But, in the meantime, everything will have been lost which had been gained during the half-century before; and, soon after the civil strife is settled, it will be ready to break out again."

The halting attitude which he was wont to assume when confronted by wide generalizations, may be illustrated by his view of the great principle that representation ought to be coextensive with taxation. It is plain that, as every one, directly or indirectly, pays taxes, the principle, pressed to its extreme conclusions, would give manhood and womanhood, if not what may be termed *childhood*, suffrage to every inhabitant, civilized or uncivilized, of our entire Indian and Colonial empire; and that it would lead to the parcelling out of the empire into equal electoral districts. It will doubtless be objected that the franchise should not be given to incompetent persons. But, in truth, this qualification is an all-important one. That, in strict theory, the franchise ought to be given to every taxpayer, but that, in practice, it should be withheld from unfit persons, and *that the present holders of power are to be judges of their unfitness*,—this is a principle to which the highest Tory need not demur.

After we had touched on these points, Pattison said thoughtfully: "In fact, it comes to this,—the principle will not bear examination." Nevertheless, he doubtless thought that the old Whigs acted wisely in assuming the correctness of this exaggerated ideal as a basis for carrying the Reform Bill, and that future reformers will have to follow their example. Indeed, he approvingly quoted an Aristotelian maxim to the effect that, when we would obtain a little from mankind, it is often needful to ask for a great deal.

He brought a like spirit to bear on the question of nationality. "The age of patriotism," he said, "is passing away, and the age of cosmopolitanism is taking its place." Irish Home Rule was not to his liking; and he regarded the cry "Egypt for the Egyptians" as, if not a *reductio ad absurdum*, at least a natural sequel of the cry "Ireland for the Irish." On my asking whether he was not of opinion that the Irish Land Bill was opposed to the principles of political economy, as those principles used to be commonly understood, he interrupted me by saying, "Of course, it is confiscation." Yet he was not prepared to deny that, in the present state of public opinion, the Bill was inevitable. It should be added that he regretted the sympathy shown by some Oxford Liberals for Lord Beaconfield's foreign policy.

In a word, he was a Whig, and not a Jingo.

It may be instructive to observe that between Pattison and Charles Austin there were many points of comparison and a few of contrast. The chief difference between them was, that Pattison had far less political and patriotic enthusiasm than Austin had. Austin (as his brother told me), shortly before he died, went to a public meeting at St. James's Hall, where the band suddenly struck up the *Marseillaise*. He had long since laid aside his juvenile sympathy with the French Revolution; yet, on hearing the old familiar strain, he rose from his seat (old and infirm as he was), and the tears came to his eyes. Personally I never saw him thus give way to his feelings; but I remember his saying that he pitied the man whose spirit was not stirred by the cry for deliverance in the *Persæ*:—

$$\text{Ὦ παῖδες Ἑλλήνων, ἴτε,}$$
$$\text{ἐλευθεροῦτε πατρίδ', ἐλευθεροῦτε δὲ}$$
$$\text{παῖδας, γυναῖκας, θεῶν τε πατρῴων ἕδη.}$$

Pattison, so far as I could judge, had hardly a spark of this patriotic zeal. His want of interest in the politics of the day is well shown by a habit of his, which is reported to me at first hand. He never turned to the newspapers till 9 p.m., and then chiefly from a sense of duty.* Generally, instead of reading them himself, he would lie down on his sofa, take out his watch, and shut his eyes, while his niece looked down the columns, and gave him the shortest possible epitome of the *Times*. If she got through it in less than twenty minutes, she was commended. But he liked to hear, at least, the heading of everything; and, if any event was afterwards mentioned which she had overlooked, he would say reproachfully, "I suppose that was not in our copy."

We once talked over the romantic visit paid to Greece by the statesman whom the Greeks called ὁ φιλέλλην καὶ περίφημος Γλάδστων. In the conversation, a passage from the Acharnians was applied to the visit—

Περικλέης οὐλύμπιος
ἤστραπτεν, ἐβρόντα, ξυνεκύκα τὴν Ἑλλάδα.

Pattison seemed pleased with the quotation, and begged to hear it again. In referring to the modern Pericles (scholar, orator, reformer), he acknowledged that he had little sympathy with him; adding, "It is strange that he is the living representative of the Liberal cause, the cause of

---

* He told a friend that he did not like to have the news "hot"—he preferred giving it time to cool. According to Goethe, you may often with advantage delay reading newspapers, as to-morrow's news may correct to-day's.

wisdom and righteousness throughout all time." On my asking whether some share of the credit was not due to the Conservative party on the ground that it *cunctando restituit rem*, he merely answered, " Sir Stafford Northcote is the representative of everything which distinguishes Englishmen from Americans." This damning with faint praise may prepare my readers for his having said, in his half-jesting way, "Though I am always abusing the Liberals, I call myself a Liberal, *and I am one*." He expressed his regret at the death of the Prince Consort by saying that it was as great a misfortune as a ten-years' innings of the Conservative party. He was told of a very lukewarm Liberal who said that, so far as the society is concerned, he would rather belong to the Carlton than to the Reform Club. "He is quite right," said the Rector; "Reformers are generally so rough and rude. Of course, the Whigs of Holland House were exceptions. But, as a general rule, my advice is *to live with the Tories and to vote with the Whigs*." A cynic might add that those who purpose following this advice, would be wise in taking full advantage of the Ballot, and not letting their High Tory friends suspect that they vote against them.

His Liberalism did not incline him to what is called the Birmingham School. In reference to an eminent writer and editor who has become a strong Radical, he said: "He has taken so much pains about *l'art d'écrire*, that he has not left himself time to acquire *l'art de vivre*. The two arts are very different, and the one often unfits a man for the other." I asked him whether De Tocqueville had not stated too broadly that the advent of democracy was inevitable. "Since he died," answered the Rector, "everything seems to be fulfilling his predictions. Nothing can stop the movement. The more you give the people, the more they will want." I called his attention to an assertion of Mr. Herbert Spencer to the effect, that the time will come when one man will not be suffered to enjoy, without working, that which another man works for without enjoying; and I asked him whether such a state of public opinion would not exclude domestic service, and, indeed, all social inequalities. "I fear it must be so," he replied. "Everything seems to be tending towards Socialism. *I hate it.*" I asked why, if so great an evil is approaching, he and those who think with him do not try to stop it. "Look there," he said, pointing to the sea at Biarritz. "Just as men can construct moles and breakwaters against the waves, so individuals can, in some slight degree, modify passing events. They are as powerless against the tide of history, as they are against the tide of the ocean. No; what is to be, will be, in spite of you and me."

It may be well to insert the epitome of a conversation which sets forth the Rector's manner of dealing with this subject, though it shows him in an unusual attitude — an attitude of defence. I reminded him that in one of his writings he had expressed a view (seemingly shared by Hallam) that Englishmen were, on the whole, better off in the reign of George II. than either before or since. He told me that he had been taken to task for this assertion, but he seemed prepared to defend it, and also to predict that England would go on declining. I insisted that, in discussing the question, we must start with the assumption that there is more good than evil in life. "I don't see," he exclaimed, "why I should assume anything of the sort; I think I shall take up the view of Schopenhauer." I recalled to him some of the conclusions that may be drawn from that wildly anti-social theory—such conclusions, for instance, as the following: Ought not these very numerous persons who say that they would not, if they could, live their lives over again—in other words, that, so far as their experience goes, the good of life is a *minus* quantity,—ought not these Schopenhauerites to rejoice instead of sorrowing at the sight or news of a shipwreck? "Well," he said, "suppose I grant that life is a good, what has that to say to human progress?" "For convenience of figures," I answered, "let us compare the present time with a time when the population of England was one-third of what it now is, and let us suppose that the average Englishman was twice as happy as now—even on this extreme supposition, the aggregate of happiness in England would be half as great again now as then; Englishmen, in tripling their numbers, would have gained more collectively than they have lost individually." "Yes, yes," he said, with amused impatience, "but this is not what is generally meant by progress." I never could draw him further than this on the optimistic path. Indeed, he seemed generally half to expect, as the most eminent of French critics half expects,* that, when reformers have done their perfect work, the world, destitute of variety and originality, will become a sort of universal China — a lubberland of lotos-eaters. Nor could he fail to see the inferences that might be drawn from such a prognostication. A great living philologist has expressed the opinion that the classical languages and literatures paid for their temporary splendour by their premature

---

* Scherer—*Etudes*, Vol. v. pp 316, 317 (on Renan), and Vol vii. p. 64 (on Carlyle).

decay. If it is likewise true that all civilization tends to decay, analogy might warrant the conjecture that patriotic and philanthropic zealots are, so to say, making the world live its life too fast, and hurrying it on to its senile decrepitude. If so, it is not a mere *counsel of imperfection* fitted for men of the world, a mere concession to the hardness of their hearts, but the highest Utilitarian ideal, that is embodied in the suggestion of the most philosophical of our judges, that perhaps " the respectable man . . . who led an easy life will turn out to have been right after all, and enthusiastic believers of all creeds to have been quite wrong." I enunciate this violent paradox, not as expressing the settled convictions of any one, but as furnishing a sample of a class of doubts which, more or less consciously, present themselves to men like Pattison, and effectually deprive them, if not of the enthusiasm of humanity, at least of what may be termed the enthusiasm of progress.

We have before stated that Pattison was not, as indeed no one can be, a consistent pessimist. By urging on education and other reforms, he showed that he was practically a believer in progress. Yet, even as a believer in progress, he was perplexed by ethical puzzles which differ from the pessimistic ones, but are hardly less embarrassing. He was amused or troubled—amused as the only alternative of being troubled—by such ἀπορίαι as the following: Would not an ideal philanthropist allow himself only the minimum of relaxation that might be necessary for the greatest efficiency of his work? Would he not sell his gold watch and take third-class railway tickets, so as to have more money to spare for the Anti-Mendicity Society and the Cancer Hospital? Ought not the passionate lover, before putting the momentous question, to satisfy himself, not merely that he has the means to support a family, but also that the population of the world stands in need of an increase? Ought we not, when ill, to forsake the medical Philistine who would treat us simply with a view to our own cure, and to resort to the nobler practitioner who would experiment on us for the good of posterity? To this last question, Pattison laughingly objected that the "neighbour" whom we are commanded to love as ourselves, cannot mean the unborn; but he knew full well that to laugh was not to solve the riddle. He knew also that these difficulties are increased (or nullified) by a further one, which may be regarded as a phase of *pessimism*, though it represents a novel aspect of that Protean creed. Mill insists that the Utilitarian principle should be applied, not to man only, but to the entire sentient universe; and certainly it is less easy to show that the principle ought not to be so extended, than that, if so extended, it might involve a *reductio ad euthanasiam*. May it not be argued that, from the philozoic point of view, the existence of the human race is altogether a mishap? Does the Unconstitutional Monarchy of Man minister to "the greatest happiness of the greatest number" of sentient beings (including earwigs and animalcules)? "I never could see," said the Rector, when dealing seriously with such questions, "any way of disposing of extreme cases, except by taking the matter at the other end, and asking: *What reason can you allege for the obligation of self-sacrifice?*" Perhaps it was in consequence of this fundamental doubt that he disliked, as he informed me, to label himself a Utilitarian. His friend, Henry Smith, told me that he also demurred to the designation, and for a similar reason. But, after all, the question is one of words. Charles Austin, the Utilitarian *par excellence*, sometimes avowed a logical scepticism as complete as Pattison's; more often, he expressed an opinion different in appearance, but substantially the same. Goethe has observed that a universal scepticism always takes refuge in a qualified belief. And thus there was, in fact, a latent scepticism in a remark which Austin once made: "I know of no *olbiometer:* so we must take the conventional estimate of what leads to pleasure or pain."* In other words, we must not be too logical, but must acquiesce in the moral standard of the good men and women among whom we live. This, I repeat, was Pattison's view; and, if I describe his ethical creed as Utilitarianism tempered by Pyrrhonism, I must be understood to mean no more than this. After all, if he was wrong, he was kept in countenance by the virtuous, nay, over-scrupulous poet who was remarkable for what Bagehot has called a "pleasant cynicism," and who gave a cynical turn even to such pathetic self-revelations as *Dipsychus, Amours de Voyage,* and *In the Great Metropolis.* Mr. Jowett, too, in his strictures on Casuistry, adopts a view similar to that of the best of the *Questioned Spirits,* the Spirit who cut ethical knots by exclaiming,

"I know not, I will do my duty";

and whose note was at times saddened into

"I know not, I must do as other men are doing."

---

* A similar view is very strongly expressed by Scherer, in *Etudes,* vi., p. 213 (on Sterne), and in the introduction to Amiel's *Journal,* pp. lxvi., lxvii. ("La vie exige des ménagements, j'allais dire des ruses. .... L'art de vivre, c'est de se faire une raison, de souscrire aux compromis, de se prêter aux fictions. .... La vie ne supporte pas d'être serrée de [tout] près. C'est une croûte mince sur laquelle il faut

The application of this principle may be shown by an example. "Pattison," writes one who knew him well, "was very fond of fishing, but he had grave misgivings as to the moral character of the amusement. He confessed to these, but I do not know that he allowed them to interfere with his practice." Likewise, Austin doubted the morality of field sports, and yet he preserved game for his guests. It is probable that both of these philosophers were acting against what may be termed their logical conscience; but they were not, in any ordinary sense of the word, *unconscientious*. The worst that can be said about them is, that they were of the marble of which sages are made, but not of the gold of which saints are made. Might they not have contended that they were merely conforming to a custom likely to be considered barbarous by a remote posterity, and that, if we would conform to no custom likely to be so regarded, we (in St. Paul's phrase) "must needs go out of the world"?*

It will now be understood what I meant when I represented the Rector's cynicism as wholly unlike the vulgar cynicism of less analytical minds.

marcher sans appuyer; donner du talon dedans, vous ferez un trou où vous disparaîtrez.")

* My view is further illustrated in *Safe Studies*, pp. 230—234. See also p. 287, note.

From the premise, *Omnia exeunt in absurdum*, he drew the conclusion, *Omnia vanitas*. He feared moral and religious enthusiasm, for he knew not whither it might lead. In the "Memoirs" he remarks quaintly—very quaintly for a clergyman—that "Religion is a good servant, but a bad master," which is the exact equivalent of Goethe's famous aphorism: "Religion is not an end, but a means, to lead us through the purest tranquillity of mind to the highest culture." In like manner, he felt that *Imperat aut servit recti mens conscia cuique*. He was (to use his own phrase) "haunted by the ideal, and baffled by philosophical perplexities,"—haunted and baffled all the more painfully, because others, far inferior to him in intellect, rose, through being unweighted by those perplexities, to a somewhat Pharisaical ideal—because they, not having tasted of the Tree of Knowledge, ate and condemned him for not eating of the Tree of Life. This being duly considered, it will be found that his sceptical, caustic, and jaunty sayings generally leave in the mouth no taste save that of a tonic bitter. We may, therefore, without scruple, give a few more examples of the cynicism which so belonged to him that one almost missed it if ever he laid it aside.

We will begin with an aphorism of his which may have been suggested by Mill's well-known statement that in England the upper classes for the most part do not lie, and that the lower classes, though almost habitually liars, are generally ashamed of lying. "Englishmen," said Pattison, "lie as much as foreigners; but Englishmen have a dim consciousness that they are lying, while foreigners believe all the while that they are telling the truth." This preferring of conscious guilt to guilt born of self-deceit, will at once recall Aristotle's comparison between ἀκρασία and ἀκολασία, and perhaps is not wholly unlike St. Paul's comparison between doing wrong things and having pleasure in them that do them. I remember asking Charles Austin if he did not think that too much fuss was made when a late Bishop of Durham appointed a highly respectable son-in-law to a good living. Being in a paradoxical vein, he answered: "What I mind is, not the thing that was done, but the sanctimonious way in which it was done. If Ben Stanley had done anything of the kind, he would have written in big letters in his diary, *This is a job*, and that would not have been half as bad. I should not hate Torquemada so much if I did not know that he was thoroughly convinced that he was doing his duty." Carlyle has paid Frederic the equivocal compliment that, although he often deceived others, he never deceived himself.

Pattison was coaching an undergraduate in the *Ethics*. The pupil, perplexed by Aristotle's reasoning, embarrassed his teacher by his importunate desire to understand it. At last Pattison said tartly: "Never mind understanding it, only get it up." The pupil was naturally hurt by this unpleasant rebuke; which, however, probably meant that the time was short, and that, if the pupil insisted on discussing first principles, instead of merely learning the answers which would satisfy the examiners, he might be disappointed in his degree, as Pattison himself had been. Nevertheless, Pattison's impatience may have been partly due to want of sympathy with the subject. When I knew him, and when he wrote his *Memoirs*, he was an Aristotelian. But he was originally a Platonist, and it was only by slow degrees that the influence of Oxford wrought the change in him. Many years ago, when speaking of the late Dr. Jeune as a successful man of the world whom he disliked, he said, "I divide men into those who love Plato and those who do not; Jeune, I am certain, does not."

When a new edition of Shakespeare came out, he said to a friend, "Instead of bringing out these old plays, why don't the editors write new ones?" My informant understood him to mean that the prevalent Shakespearolatry is a mere delusion. If he really held this opinion, he had given it up when he wrote his *Life of Milton*, and when I knew him. He told me, however, that he thought that there is much exaggeration in the popular judgment on the subject, and that the great excellence of Shakespeare is to be sought in the beautiful passages that abound in his plays, rather than in his power of delineating character. He took greater delight in reading the Sonnets than the Plays; he found fault with *Romeo and Juliet*, and even *The Tempest* was not one of his favourites. Every old man, says Goethe, is a King Lear. It is characteristic of Pattison that he regarded *King Lear* and *Père Goriot* as superior in tragic interest to any other modern works of fiction.

He certainly used odd language about poets. In an article on Tennyson, I had contrasted the poet with more mature thinkers. Pattison wrote to me: "The phrase, 'more mature thinkers,' implies that Tennyson is a thinker at all. Is he so? Is he not a poet, and are not poets and thinkers incompatibles?" This can only have meant that a poet, *quâ* poet, is not a thinker, and that it would go hardly even with the greatest poets if we subjected their reasoning to the severe test which we apply to the reasoning of philosophers. Hamlet's soliloquy assuredly could not bear that test.

"The religion of uneducated [unphilosophical] persons is the same everywhere, and has been the same since the foundation of the world." This oracular sentence was addressed by Pattison to a brother clergyman who, though a Broad Churchman, was rather shocked by it. Its meaning (so far as it has any) probably resembles that of Charles Austin's favourite quotation—the line in which the Tory and orthodox Dryden affirms that "priests of all religions are the same."

One is sometimes startled, after knowing one corner of a great man's mind well, to find how many corners there are of which one knew nothing. In my intercourse with Pattison, I never suspected that he took an interest in otter-hunting and horse-racing. The latter taste is well illustrated by the following anecdote, communicated to me by one of his pupils :—

"The year of the great match between *Voltigeur* and *Flying Dutchman*, he suddenly asked me, which horse would win. I answered calmly : 'It depends on the state of the ground; the *Dutchman* is the faster horse, but, if the ground is heavy, *Voltigeur* will win.' He seemed delighted with such an answer from a 'slow' man, but the question followed, 'How did you learn that?' 'Oh, I talked it over with the coachman on the box as I came up,' and his countenance fell."

During his lifetime I never dreamt that his proficiency in croquet was such that he aspired to become Champion of all England. But I knew that he took an interest in the game. This came out in an odd way. On my mentioning the name of a lady who is a strong advocate of Women's Rights, he exclaimed eagerly, " I know something of Miss ———. She was playing at croquet, and I was acting as head of the side. When it was her turn, I told her not to try to go through the hoop, but merely to place her ball in front of it. She replied stiffly, 'Thank you, I would rather play my own game.' She tried to go through the hoop, missed it, and the game was lost. I said to myself, *That girl has an undisciplined mind.*"

One evening, the Rector, as he was wishing me good-night, told me rather mysteriously that he was going the next day to call on the Editor of the *Times* (Mr. Chenery). I asked whether he thought him an able man. Not being in a communicative mood, he answered, "Do you know that you are putting a very hard question? It is just as if you asked me—well—whether I think Jupiter clever," and he laughed as he hurried away.

He liked novel reading, and it was a sort of affectation with him to seem to like it a great deal (as might perhaps have been inferred from the last sentence in the *Life of Milton*). Being asked whether a former pupil, who was making his mark in the world, kept up his taste for literature, he answered, " Yes, he reads all the novels that come out, *and he remembers them too.*" He declared (how seriously I know not) that he preferred contemporary French literature (including novels) to contemporary English literature. Nor was this the only respect in which he was wont to depreciate the intellectual atmosphere of England. A friend writes :—

"He spoke once somewhat bitterly of the treatment of public men, and men of energy, in England. He said, 'If a man was a country squire and did nothing, just lived an easy, good-tempered sportsman's life, all men spoke well of him, and he was popular, and life was made pleasant for him; immediately a man showed energy and worked, he was thwarted, calumny begun, and he became unpopular. It was so with statesmen, and so with the Bishops. The Bishops who did nothing were liked; Wilberforce (then of Oxford, about 1849-50), who showed some energy, was calumniated and hated by many, and anything was believed against him.'"

Was Pattison also thinking of the contrast between the French admiration for Richelieu and the English abhorrence of Strafford?

A trifling incident may show how strong was his antipathy to the narrow classical instruction which used to form the chief staple of our public school education. I had been talking about my own school-time at Harrow. He turned round and asked abruptly, "Did you learn anything there?" I hesitated. "Answer me, *Yes* or *No*. Can you recall a single thing worth remembering that you learnt during all the years that you spent there?" I replied that, owing to my extreme short sight and consequent slowness in looking out words in a dictionary, I was not a good sample of a Harrow boy, but that some of my schoolfellows certainly learnt much. "Yes," he said, doubtfully, " perhaps you may be right."

He upbraided me in a sort of semi-banter, because in the *Fortnightly Review* I praised Charles Austin for continuing, when failing health drove him from the Bar, to do what active work he could as Chairman of Quarter Sessions. "Do you know, I feel quite hurt by your saying this? Can you seriously mean that the βίος πρακτικός is superior to the βίος θεωρητικός? I can hardly conceive anything more dreadful than for such a man as Austin to have wasted his time over the drudgery of Quarter Sessions." This is pitched in the same key as the opinion of Goethe, quoted both by Hayward and by Pattison, that "a purely poetical subject is as superior to a political one, as the pure everlasting truth of Nature is to party spirit."

I called the Rector's attention to a very Pattisonian confession of Sainte-Beuve, who seemed to limit his moral aspirations to "un composé de bonnes habitudes, de bonnes manières, d'honnêtes procédés, reposant d'ordinaire sur un fonds plus ou moins généreux, sur une nature plus ou moins bien née;" and I asked him whether the last two words mean *well constituted* (in the sense which Mr. Galton deems so important) or *well-born* (as opposed to *risen from the ranks*). He answered that the latter was the meaning; and, after mentioning a very distinguished self-made man (lately deceased), he put the query, "Could anything have turned him into a gentleman?"

After he had delivered his lecture at Bedford College in 1883, I suggested that he should send it to a new and struggling periodical with which I knew that he warmly sympathized. He answered that the application had already been made by the editor: "It was asking me to make him a present of £25, to which my μεγαλοπρέπεια was not equal. I know I ought to be content with the approval of the Dean of St. Paul's, who wrote to me, 'Nothing so true and so real has been said for a long time'; but I also remember the text, Εἰ ἐν τῷ ἀδίκῳ μαμμωνᾷ πιστοὶ οὐκ ἐγένεσθε, τὸ ἀληθινὸν τίς ὑμῖν πιστεύσει;" He therefore intended to send the revised lecture to a popular magazine, but his intention seems to have been relinquished through failing health. This sounds very mercenary; but, if he had not been a ἑαυτὸν τιμωρούμενος and a ἑαυτοῦ κατηγορῶν, he would have said, and with substantial truth, that his reason for declining the request was a desire to exert an influence over the greatest possible number of readers. I do not blame him for thus writing to me in the cynical dialect, as he knew that I should translate his words into the vernacular. But it is certainly unfortunate that he often used the same dialect, a dialect very open to misconstruction, in addressing persons almost certain to misconstrue it.

A former pupil of Pattison, an orthodox divine, who, though very well off, continues to take an active part in education, told me that the Rector once said to him,—" You are the most ungrateful man in the world. Providence has given you the opportunity of being idle, and you won't take advantage of it." I am sorry that I never asked Pattison whether, in giving this most uncharacteristic advice, he was not thinking of Gibbon's paradox that the vices of the clergy are less dangerous than their virtues—whether, in fact, he was not resorting to an "economy of truth" in the hope of inducing his very ecclesiastical friend to leave education alone. If this was not his meaning, the admonition must have been one of those *counsels of imperfection* to which I have alluded. It is simply impossible that the advice to seek delights and shun laborious days would be given by the censor who has denounced the entire generation of middle-aged Oxford dons as stricken with intellectual palsy. His state of mind was, perhaps, similar to Renan's: "Tout en étant fort appliqué, je me demande sans cesse si ce ne sont pas les gens frivoles qui ont raison." I call attention to this passage, as it is about as good an example as could be given of that *importunateness* of memory and reflection which is (so to say) the presiding demon of analytical thought.

The gospel of idleness is merely a part of the gospel of self-indulgence; and the grain of salt which is needed to make the former gospel palatable, or even tolerable, must now be added for the seasoning of the latter. If the following saying of Pattison, the most cynical that I shall quote, can be more or less satisfactorily interpreted, all his cynical sayings can be so interpreted. In *Safe Studies*, p. 187, I enunciate the truism that husband and wife should comfort and sustain one another in struggling for the good of all men. In page 116, I quote with disapproval a strange assertion of Montaigne, "He who abandons his own healthful and pleasant life to serve others, takes, in my opinion, a course that is wrong and unnatural." Concerning these contradictory maxims Pattison wrote: "In page 187, will you stand to the words 'for the good of all men'? Do you not much rather incline to endorse Montaigne's opinion, p. 116, a refreshing passage, to which I wish I had the reference in the original?" In this frank avowal we seem to hear an echo of the "Unjust Voice" in the *Clouds*:—

Σκέψαι γὰρ, ὦ μειράκιον, ἐν τῷ σωφρονεῖν ἅπαντα
Ἄνεστιν, ἡδονῶν θ' ὅσων μέλλεις ἀποστερεῖσθαι,
Παίδων, γυναικῶν, κοττάβων, ὄψων, πότων, κιχλισμῶν.
Καίτοι τί σοι ζῆν ἄξιον, τούτων ἐὰν στερηθῇς;
Neph. 1071—5.

But, on the other hand, Pattison was often on the side of the *Just Voice*, sometimes in an extreme degree. I remember pleading for that modified eccentricity, that social independence, which was so dear to the heart of Mill. Pattison, himself not the most conventional of men,* surprised me by objecting, "Eccentricity seems to me a form of egoism, and all egoism ought to be discouraged." This little sermon of his may help us to draw the sting from his Apology for Montaigne. Let us observe that in that Apology he uses the word "refreshing," which shows that

* For example: after he had only once met Miss Swanwick, he (having, I suppose, chanced to dine in the neighbourhood) sent up his card one evening between 9 and 10, and asked if she could receive him. She was glad to avail herself of the opportunity to renew their classical discussions, but was amused at the hour chosen by her untimely guest.

he stood in need of refreshment—that, in fact he relished Montaigne's aphorism as an anodyne under an oppressive sense of the social martyrdom to which ethical logic might lead. In practice, no doubt, he would have differed from Mill in assigning the limits of self-sacrifice; but, theoretically, his paradoxical words *perhaps* mean no more than Mill would have expressed by saying that, in our present low state of civilization, we cannot ignore the necessity of loving ourselves and those near to us better than those more remote. They *certainly* mean no more than Professor Bain (on *The Study of Character*) has expressed by saying that disinterestedness is " an exception to the only sane principle of conduct, which is, for every being to look to its own pleasures and pains—a brilliant exception, it is true, something of the *splendide mendax*, but never to be made the rule without even suicidal consequences."

We may sum up our view of the Rector's cynicism by affirming that he

"laughed that any one should weep
In this disjointed world for one wrong more."

Or, more shortly, we may say of him, as of Democritus, that he laughed to prevent weeping. Mr. Greg has quaintly remarked that *hardly any one* can afford to keep a conscience, that is, a strictly logical one. He might have maintained that *no one* can afford such a luxury. Clough, whose poetry the Rector (strange to say) did not appreciate, puts the case yet more strongly :—

> " We cannot act without assuming x,
> And at the same time y, its contradictory;
> *Ergo*, to act."*

To a sensitive nature like Pattison's, these Antinomies of the Practical Reason are at times not a curious enigma, but a painful reality. A person thus constituted can enter into Scherer's experience that *Nous cotoyons l'abîme, gare au vertige*. He has learnt that the strivings of his abnormal conscience towards its goal often need, not stimulating, but checking; and his cynical utterances, harsh and unnatural in their tone, are naught but the grating sound of the drag which is put on the wheel.

In referring to the father of all sceptics, whose treatise by means of a felicitous forgery has made its way into the Canon of Scripture, Renan oddly remarks : " La bonté du sceptique est la plus solide de toutes ; elle repose sur un sentiment profond

---

* See also the fifth stanza of *The Higher Courage*. In *The Latest Decalogue*, the contrast is marked between ideal and conventional morality :—

> " Thou shalt not covet, but tradition
> Approves all forms of competition."

de la vérité suprême, *Nil expedit.*"* I pointed out this sentence to Pattison, who seemed to regard it with something of approval. But he would doubtless have admitted that the word *bonté* must be referred rather to public than to private virtue—must be taken to denote not *heroism,* but *kindliness.* So interpreted, the words may be applied to Pattison himself. Charles Austin was fond of a saying of Voltaire to the effect that, if one would fain work for mankind, one must avoid being disgusted with mankind, and must therefore forbear seeing too much of ordinary men and women. It is perhaps safer to assert that some who devote their time and sympathy to public objects, and all who thirst after a wide popularity, impair their capacity for contracting close friendships—for making a few men and women feel that they take a personal

---

* Again, in *L'Antechrist*, p. 101, he describes *Ecclesiastes* as a "livre charmant, le seul livre aimable qui ait été composé par un Juif;" and adds (p. 102),—"Nous ne comprenons pas le galant homme sans un peu de scepticisme; nous aimons que l'homme vertueux dise de temps à autre, *Vertu, tu n'es qu'un mot.*" He goes on to say that the power of smiling at one's own work is "la qualité essentielle d'une personne distinguée," and maintains that this quality was strikingly exemplified in Christ. I wish that some reader would inform me what saying or sayings of Christ, Renan could possibly have had in his mind when he made this startling assertion.

interest in them. Pattison achieved this, though he laboured under a great drawback. Study engrossed much of his time and interest; and, perhaps on that account, he was at the close of his life lacking in power of sympathy. May it not have been because his small disposable fund of time and sympathy was seldom drawn upon for mankind in the aggregate, that he had any time or sympathy to spare for the few women and fewer men whom he really valued? At any rate, his misanthropy, or rather his *aphilanthropy*, freed him from that last infirmity of noble reformers—intolerance of human frailty. Other causes might be mentioned; but the foregoing may serve to explain how it was that the Rector enjoyed the privilege—a privilege rarely vouchsafed to such a hard student—of inspiring the few whom he admitted to his friendship with a larger measure of, not admiration merely, but affection. It may not be amiss to record a curious instance of the enthusiasm which he once excited in an unexpected quarter. One of his old pupils writes: "For part of my time, Pattison's scout was also mine. He was the only honest, manly, true-hearted man as a college scout that I ever knew, and he almost adored Pattison." One fact may serve to explain the scout's devotion to his master. Pattison strongly disapproved of the complete separation which, in English households especially, subsists between masters and servants. When sociably inclined, he made spasmodic attempts to break through the barrier.

It was with some surprise that I learnt at Biarritz how unknown Pattison was, even by name, to most of the travelling English. There was something at once instructive and humbling in the question that I heard asked, "Do you know that there is a brother of Sister Dora in the hotel?"—implying that he was doomed to Lethe, and that no one but his sister could rescue him even for a short space (*Juturnam misero succurrere fratri*). Being consulted by an undergraduate as to what he should do in the way of study, Pattison startled his questioner by answering (in effect), "Take care of *what you are*, and *what you do* will take care of itself." The world is happily determined to apply this principle to Pattison,—to judge him, not by what he did, but by what he was, and not to let him be written down even by himself. One of his kinsfolk, who had ample means of judging, assures me that his disappointment in 1851 "weighed upon his memory" far more during his last illness than it had done for many years before. He had, in fact, lived to become a mere—

ἄθλιον
εἴδωλον, οὐ γὰρ δὴ τόδ' ἀρχαῖον δέμας.

This may partly explain the defects of his *Memoirs*; for it is, I think, just as well as generous to refer in great measure to his morbid condition the deplorable domestic and academic disclosures, and the more deplorable exaggerations about Conington which deface that unfortunate volume.*

> "If 't be so,
> Hamlet is of the faction that is wronged,
> His madness is poor Hamlet's enemy."

The Rector was never very misanthropical when talking to me; perhaps he thought misanthropy would not be good for me. Shortly after we parted at Biarritz, he wrote about me to a lady friend (the inscription is *bilingual*, being on a post-card):—" Pray present my compliments to our *philosophe errant*, and prevail upon him to se

---

* So far from becoming a bigoted Puseyite after his "conversion," Conington was to the last very tolerant. I asked him (in or about 1857) what he thought of a contemptuous attack on Mr. Congreve which had recently appeared in the *Times*. He replied that he liked far better an article in the *Saturday Review*, which, while differing from Mr. Congreve's views, treated him with consideration. On another occasion, one of his Liberal friends (some of his friends were strong Liberals) informed him in my presence that I had ventured to tell that Tory assembly, the Oxford Union, that we owed a debt of gratitude to Carlyle for importing into England a taste for German theology. Conington merely looked at me and said, with an amused smile, "Really, really." I have elsewhere recorded his great admiration for Mill.

détendre un peu plus, if he wishes to keep the machine in good order." It may have been with a like feeling of goodwill that, knowing or fancying that I am wont to take too grave and sad a view of human life, he put (so to speak) into his conversation with me little of the spirit of Timon and much of the spirit of Montaigne; just as Horace infused into Odes addressed to the comrades of his youth a mild Epicureanism as an antidote to Republican zeal.

Thirteen years ago, I asked a distinguished Oxonian to tell me whom he thought the foremost man in the University. "Jowett," he replied, "has a touch of genius, which Pattison has not; otherwise, taking him all round, Pattison is the first man in Oxford." I would venture to add that (still perhaps excepting Mr. Jowett) he was the first clergyman of our time. Not, of course, that his tastes were those of his clerical brethren. A Scotch book called *Natural Law in the Spiritual World*, which has had a "mad success" with old maids, clergymen, and homœopathic doctors, was sent to him, perhaps in order to convert him. Not relishing its author's *naïve* attempt to keep the newest wine in cracked bottles, and also to found on the wholesale immorality of natural forces analogies such as might more consistently be used to defend the religion of Juggernaut than the religion of Jesus, he said drily to a friend, "I don't think this book will suit us," and contemptuously threw it aside.* In talking with him one day, I expressed surprise at the almost universal obscurantism of the Bishops. "It is quite natural," he said. "After a man has been consecrated ten years, he loses all sympathy with the modern spirit. No; there is one exception. The Bishop of —— sometimes sits next me at luncheon at the Athenæum,† and asks simple questions, just like a little boy, about evolution and other modern speculations. This Bishop really tries to keep pace with the modern spirit; but he is the only one." He, however, emphatically pronounced Dean Stanley to be a "thorough Liberal," a circumstance which seemed to surprise him on account of the Dean's imaginative and perhaps unscientific cast of mind. Pattison's summary condemnation of the Anglican Bishops was probably meant to be taken more or less in jest. But he was speaking quite seriously when

* A writer in the *Contemporary Review* for March passes a yet severer judgment on the book; he stigmatizes its author's theory as "neither science nor theology, but a bastard Calvinism of which Scotland ought to be ashamed." Is *legitimate* Calvinism much better?

† The Rector said that the library of the Athenæum "is the most delightful place in the world—especially on a Sunday morning."

he pronounced a very similar judgment on a far more formidable body of ecclesiastics. I asked him whether he did not expect that, at no distant period, some wise Pope and Cardinals will (by a now familiar device) seek to disburden Catholicism of the belief in hell—whether, in fact, they will not demonstrate that the Popes who sanctioned that unsavoury doctrine were not speaking *ex cathedrâ*, or were misreported, or that the question lies beyond the province of Papal Infallibility; or, at any rate, that *Nullum tempus occurrit Deo* (see 2 Peter iii., 8), and that every expedient which is used to show that the numerous plain texts which seem to predict the immediate end of the world do not really mean what they seem to mean, will equally show that the texts and other Catholic authorities which seem to predict the endlessness of hell need not mean what they seem to mean.* "No," replied he; "Catholicism will not change. The Cardinals have no conception whatever of the intellectual changes going on in the world. They often show ability in diplomatic matters, but in nothing else." Yet, though untainted by the ecclesiastical virus, he was to the last a clergyman in the best sense.

* Tillotson (*l.c.*), after quoting Jonah iii. 10, to prove that God may be better than his word, raises the delicious question: Would he also be better than his oath (Ps. xcv. 11)?

He rather surprised a friend by making the broad statement that mankind will never be able to dispense with religious observances. He was thereupon reminded that "never" is a far-reaching word, and was asked whether he did not think that, at some very remote epoch, the temptations to crime may be so much lessened, and public opinion may be so much better organized, that morality will be able to stand on its own bottom. "I accept the correction," he answered frankly; "such a time *may* come; but, if it ever is to come, it is now so extremely distant that we and our children will only get into trouble by taking it into practical consideration."

My readers may remember Pattison's observation that the idea of Deity has now been "defecated to a pure transparency."* This queer metaphor will serve as an introduction to his views on the two foundation-stones of Natural Theology. I asked him whether he thought that either Mr. Stopford Brooke or Mr. Voysey is likely to have much permanent influence. He answered in the negative; in the present state of opinion, most of those whose temperament leads them to reject what Mr. Stopford Brooke and Mr. Voysey agree in rejecting, will not accept what

* Quoted by Mr. Harrison, *Nineteenth Century*, Vol. xv., p. 496.

they agree in accepting. In short, the stream of tendency is towards Agnosticism. I asked what he thought of the logical strength of Agnosticism; and, by way of drawing him out, I stated as forcibly as I could the argument which Mr. Grote —the "rigid Atheist," as he was called in Benthamite circles—would certainly have used against it. Mr. Grote would have insisted that there is not a tittle of evidence to show that fairies do not exist, and yet that, as soon as it became manifest that there is no evidence to show that they do exist, the case went against them by default; we do not merely *doubt* their existence, we *deny* it. In like manner, Mr. Grote applied to all spiritual beings the maxim that *Entia non sunt multiplicanda praeter necessitatem*, and he would have contended that, just as Unitarianism has been called a feather bed to catch a falling Christian, even so Agnosticism is a feather bed to catch a falling Theist.* When I laid this reason-

* An eminent jurist and philosopher, after reading this paragraph, asked me how we could possibly *deny* the existence of fairies. I answered that by the word "fairies" I mean spiritual beings able and willing to act in a specified manner on human affairs. If junkets mysteriously disappear, their owner unhesitatingly attributes the disappearance to thieves, mice, or some other natural agency; in other words, he denies that there exists any "fairy Mab" able and willing to steal junkets. In like manner, we may confidently deny that there exists a Spiritual Being who is able and willing

ing before Pattison, I found to my amazement that it was quite unfamiliar to him. In answer to it, he merely quoted with approval the words of a Greek sage (I think Protagoras): Θεοὶ εἰ εἰσὶν ἢ εἰ μὴ εἰσὶν ἄδηλον.

An Oxford contemporary and friend of Pattison's, the late Sir Benjamin Brodie, used to quote approvingly a very similar passage from Faust:—

> "Wer darf ihn nennen?
> Und wer bekennen:
> Ich glaub' ihn?
> Wer empfinden
> Und sich unterwinden
> Zu sagen: Ich glaub' ihn nicht?"

It may serve to throw light on the Rector's state of mind, and perhaps, too, on the theological tendencies of the University, if I advert for a moment to Brodie's opinions on these subjects. He called himself an A. L. (Advanced Liberal). Like Pattison, he was sceptical about miracles. In rebuking a friend whom he deemed too credulous, he exclaimed, "You'll tell me next that you believe that the serpent climbed up the tree and began talking to Eve." Yet he told me that Comte's *Positive Philosophy* seemed to "throw a wet blanket" over him; and he rather startled to modify Natural Laws, even with a view to the prevention of sin and sorrow.

me by expressing regret at the line taken by Professor Tyndall in the *Belfast Address*. He insisted that Berkeley's Theory has never been refuted (though I doubt whether the Bishop would have acknowledged him as a disciple). His meaning probably was that, while believing in the absolute uniformity of Natural Laws, he yet thought (as Mr. Romanes thinks) that the ultimate *causa causarum*, the basis of phenomena, may be Spiritual and Intelligent. "The real puzzle is," he used to say, "how *anything* comes to exist,"—anything whatever, either Mind or Matter. He once expressed a belief or hope that the course of Nature is directed by "Infinite Wisdom"; and, on being asked how he reconciled Infinite Wisdom with the existence of evil, he replied that we do not quite know what the word "infinite" means. These opinions of the late Professor of Chemistry are more optimistic than those commonly expressed by Pattison; but they may illustrate them by pointing to a *modus vivendi*—seemingly the only one—between Theism and modern science. Though I could not persuade either Brodie or Pattison to expound their views fully, I should conjecture that they were something of this sort:—

"Nature, indeed, is profoundly immoral; with reckless impartiality, she gives her sunstrokes to the evil and to the good, and causes her floods to descend on the just and on the unjust. Yet it is this same immoral agent which, by yielding suitable conditions, has led to the evolution of all our moral sentiments, and may lead to the evolution of yet higher moral sentiments among posterity. For aught we know, those moral sentiments could not have been evolved by any less painful process."

Yet, though Pattison refused to acquiesce in Grote's dogmatic negation, he relinquished a belief which was till lately regarded as a necessary adjunct of Theism, but which some disciples of Dr. Martineau are now prepared to give up. I reminded him of the havoc which the modern belief in the absolute uniformity of Natural Law is making with the older belief, the belief in supernatural intervention; and I asked him whether he did not feel a difficulty in reconciling the modern belief with the belief in the greatest of all miracles, the Miracle of Creation.* "Yes," he answered thoughtfully, "I suppose that Pantheism is the only form of Theism which can be reconciled with Evolution." Pantheism is an ugly word, and also a very vague one. I imagine that, in using it,

* In my *Safe Studies*, pp. 390, 391, this argument is stated more fully, almost in the words in which it wa addressed to the Rector.

Pattison merely meant to express a view identical with Goethe's:—

> "Was wär' ein Gott, der nur von aussen stiesse,
> Im Kreis das All am Finger laufen liesse,
> Ihm ziemt's die Welt im Innern zu bewegen,
> Natur in Sich, Sich in Natur zu hegen,
> So dass, was in Ihm lebt und webt und ist,
> Nie Seine Kraft, nie Seinen Geist vermisst."

As in regard to Theism, so in regard to the belief in immortality, Pattison (like Renan) declined to deduce the negative conclusion which some might have drawn from his premisses. He spoke indeed differently at different times. Sometimes his view seemed to be a depressing one. For instance, he once startled me with the query, "Shall I have my library in heaven?"—a question in reply to which I certainly was unable to give more definite information than he himself possessed, but which somehow conveyed the notion that he regarded a posthumous library and a posthumous life as equally improbable, or at any rate that he would find the latter tedious without the former. So, again, in a touching and mournful letter which he wrote to me three weeks before he died, he said, "I am approached very near now to the 'fabulae Manes et domus exilis Plutonia.'" And we learn with pain that, as his end drew near, the shadows became yet darker.

But he would assuredly have maintained that his real views were those which he held in the fulness of health, though even in health a man of his temperament may have forebodings that the ghost of his old belief will haunt him in the last scene,

"Pale and pitiful now, but terrible then to the dying";

in other words, that posthumous fears will overwhelm him in the sad hour when the impressions of childhood are often relatively the strongest, and when the nerves are so weakened and the thoughts are so uncontrolled that even the mightiest of spiritual reformers are tempted to utter the cry of loneliness and despair, "My God, my God, why hast thou forsaken me?"* When Pattison was at his best, his anticipations in re-

---

* Suppose an angel (or devil) were to offer us the choice between painless annihilation and the necessity of drawing from a prophetic lottery containing 1000 tickets marked *heaven* and one ticket marked *hell:* most of us, I conceive, would prefer the euthanasian alternative to the risk, the extremely small risk, of everlasting torments. And may not a dying philosopher, *whose nerves have been unstrung by illness*, be excused if he shudders at the very barest possibility that the belief in posthumous discomfort, a belief held by some persons as honest and as learned as he is, may be well founded, and if he is tempted to follow the example of the numerous penitents, from Cephalus to Littré, who at the eleventh hour

"advertunt animos ad religionem, . . .
Aeternas quoniam pœnas in morte timendum est"?

gard to immortality were such as might be resolved into the formula, *Aut caelum aut nihil;* he refused to close the door on religious hope. Goethe has well said that *Man is always more anthropomorphic than he thinks.* It is equally true—indeed, it is another aspect of the same truth—that Man is always more optimistic than he thinks. And perhaps it was in consequence of an irrepressible aspiration that a passage of Tennyson which exactly expressed Pattison's own relation to those whom he had loved and lost, suggested itself, when the news of his death came, to one at least of his sorrowing friends :—

> "It may be that the gulfs will wash us down,—
> It may be we shall touch the Happy Isles,
> And see the great Achilles whom we knew."

In conclusion, we will turn from this cheerless subject to one or two of the Rector's criticisms on life, which show him at his best. To a friend who complained that old age made our pleasures less numerous and less vivid, he answered, in a spirit worthy of Cato Major: "What we lose in the number and vividness of our pleasures, we gain in διάνοια: we set a juster value on those which remain to us."

When I saw Charles Austin for the last time, he was less of a pessimist than I had ever known him; and likewise to Pattison, just before his fatal illness began, there was vouchsafed a sort of Indian summer. He was more cheerful than usual, and yet he had a presentiment that his days were numbered. "I never," he said, "felt life to be so precious as now when it is ebbing away."* He was talking to one whom he had every reason to love and value; so he laid aside reserve and took a retrospect of his career. Enlarging on a topic which cannot but recall the choice of Solomon, he gave reasons for thinking that, if he had coveted wealth or worldly distinction, he might have secured either or both. But he had preferred the path of knowledge. "I am glad," he concluded, "that I made this choice; and, if with my present experience I could live my life over again, I would lay it out on the same lines." Adapting his Master's words, he might have said:—*Unum est necessarium. Optimam partem elegi, quae non auferetur a me.*

* He was thus confirming from personal experience a saying of Goethe's which he used often to quote: "Life resembles the Sibylline book; it becomes dearer the less there remains of it." Does not this explain the anomaly, that some permanent invalids say that they would willingly live their lives over again, while many strong persons foolishly declare that they would not? He who knows that his life is precarious, feels that it is priceless.

NOTE.

"They also serve who only stand and wait."—MILTON.

IN reference to the observations made in this article as to the interest taken by Pattison in Amiel's *Journal Intime*, M. Scherer published in the *Times* (June 2, 1885) the following letter addressed by Pattison to himself:—

"Richmond, Yorkshire, *July* 9, 1883.

"Dear Sir,—It is so long since we met that I have felt some hesitation as to addressing you by letter, lest in the crowd of new faces and figures your memory should fail to recognize me.

"The occasion of my writing is the *Journal of Amiel*, of which you are the editor. I wish to convey to you, Sir, the thanks of one at least of the public for giving the light to this precious record of a unique experience. I say unique, but I can vouch that there is in existence at least one other soul which has lived through the same struggles, mental and moral, as Amiel. In your pathetic description of the " volonté qui voudrait vouloir, mais impuissante à se fournir à elle-même des motifs "—of the repugnance for all action— the soul petrified by the sentiment of the infinite, in all this I recognise myself!

"' Celui qui a déchiffré le secret de la vie finie, qui en a lu le mot, est sorti du monde des vivants, il est mort de fait.'

"I can feel forcibly the truth of this, as it applies to myself!

"It is not, however, with the view of thrusting my egotism upon you that I have ventured upon addressing you. As I cannot suppose that so peculiar a psychological revelation will enjoy a wide popularity, I think it a duty to the editor to assure him that there are persons in the world whose souls respond, in the depths of their inmost nature, to the cry of anguish which makes itself heard in the pages of these remarkable confessions.

"Believe me to be, dear Sir, yours faithfully,
"MARK PATTISON."

I am tempted to follow M. Scherer's example by inserting a letter written by Pattison to me on receipt of my "Safe Studies." It is not without scruple that I print it even for private circulation, owing to the personal reference in the last sentence. But the whole letter seems to me instructive and characteristic of its author, and, as I have already quoted its most paradoxical and cynical expressions, it is perhaps fair to show from the context that Pattison at times used language far removed from paradox and cynicism.

"Lincoln College, Oxford, *January* 13, 1884.

"My dear Sir,—The literary event of the week has been your book—a stirring event to a sick man almost confined to his sofa. I have been reading, reading for three days, and have gone through the whole (except the Engadine), much of it more than once. The level of the collected papers stands so high, that I now regret the volume was not published—for your credit that is, since, as a collector, an unpublished volume is five times as precious to me. The material aspect of the book is worthy, in binding, paper, and type, of its author. But how could you give in to the American plan of cutting down the margin; a plan which makes it impossible to have a book bound, when its cloth cover shall be used up?

"If I may venture on a general remark, I should say that the papers, as a whole, show a union which is very uncommon, of two opposite qualities, viz., a dominant interest in speculation of a wide and human character, with vast resources in the memory, of single facts, incidents, or *mots*, of famous men. How, with your eyesight, you ever compassed such a range of reading, as is here brought to bear at all points of your argument, must be matter of wonder. It seems as if you could draw at pleasure upon all literature, from the Classics down to Robert Montgomery and Swinburne. In this respect, I desiderate references in the footnotes to the sources, that one might have the great pleasure of turning out the citations in their original place. But no doubt it would have been difficult for you, where you are, destitute of books, to have supplied these in many cases. Had I been in health I could have revelled in a notice, through many columns of the *Academy*; but, in my present condition, it is not possible for me to undertake any literary work, even of the lightest kind. If I now venture upon making some small notes upon single passages, you must not suppose that I am setting up to correct you, but am only desirous to show with what attention I have read you. In page 12, I feel a slight difficulty with the sentence which begins with the words, 'As the confusion.' The two 'its' must be relative to the noun 'confusion'; then, what is the opinion meant in the concluding words of the sentence? In page 27, I am brought up by Grote saying that the 'Geocentric theory was once as firmly held as—' Grote surely could not mean that *firmly held* is the smallest evidence of truth? The transmutation of metals and the powers of witches were equally firmly held; and we believe, or accept, the Heliocentric theory on its own evidence, and because the Geocentric theory has been proved* to be false, and not be-

---

* In what sense "proved"? In scientific matters, the very few experts of each generation form their own judgment indeed, but form it in accordance with the canons of evidence which are deemed conclusive in that generation. The very numerous inexperts, if they are sensible, follow the judgment of the experts: they follow it, however, not as infallible, but as less likely to be wrong than the judgment of any one else. This is true of the nineteenth century as well as of the sixteenth.—[L. A. T.]

cause it is firmly and universally held. In page 187, will you stand to the words of the bottom line, 'for the good of all men'? Do you not much rather incline to endorse Montaigne's opinion, quoted in page 116, a refreshing passage, to which I wish I had the reference in the original? In page 194, would not Disraeli's *mot* have gained in effect by giving it to him by name? In page 172, Chevalier Ramsay is injured by the prefix 'A certain'; he was a very well-known man in his day, just before or contemporary with Hume, and his books were the popular books of his day, especially 'Les Voyages de Cyprus,' an imitation of Telemachus, which was translated into all the languages on the Continent. He had an Oxford D.C.L. conferred upon him, but probably more in consideration of his Jacobitism—he was at one time tutor in the Pretender's family—than his literary repute. All that is related of Grote is most interesting; but I cannot forgive him for stigmatizing Paley as disingenuous, one of the most honest clergymen of the period. In page 209 the phrase 'more mature thinkers' implies that Tennyson is a thinker at all. Is he so? Is he not a poet, and are not poet and thinker incompatibles? In page 165, any young Curate or Priest who pronounced the Benediction over the head of his Bishop would be committing a gross breach of clerical etiquette. In page 180, did you notice that you were speaking of the *Quarterly Review* as a contemporary, though I suppose you intended to discard in what are now 'Studies' the original form of article? In page 223, 'the saying of a great orator' (who?) of the House of Lords that it is 'not made for perpetuity,' had already appeared on page 175.

"By this time I must have tired your patience with my trivial remarks, of which I hope you will take as little notice as they deserve. I have had to explain to everyone, to whom I have shown the book, the meaning of the title 'Safe.' It is, I say, a *vox praegnans, immo gravida, e cujus sinu proles altera, prodigiosa, periculosa, damnosa, exitura sit!* As for those people whose feet were cold because they washed them, it is no doubt quite true, but then they washed them in warm water; had they bathed them every morning in cold water, they would have been as warm as the dirty man's. That is a melancholy sentence with which your preface concludes. Though it is by no means my view that a man should be always producing books, or putting his thoughts in print, yet he cannot renounce a life which has hitherto been one of moral and philosophical discussion, without falling to a lower grade in the rational scale. For my part, I cannot expect ever to see you again; and I must be content with here recording my experience that your conversation was to me more stimulating than that of any man I ever met.—With kind regards,

"Believe me to be,
"Sincerely yours,
"Mark Pattison."

Even the far too friendly expression of opinion in the concluding sentence has a biographical value as testifying to its author's sympathetic kindliness—a quality for which, among men at least, he had little credit. In reply, I ventured to point out what seemed to me one or two oversights. For example, I explained that, when I spoke of a young Curate pronouncing the Benediction in the presence of an Archbishop, I was assuming the Archbishop not to be taking any part in the service, but merely to be one of the congregation. I touched also on private matters; and at last, with real emotion, I thanked Pattison for all his kindness and bade him farewell—

... *spargens flores et functus inani Munere.*

APPENDIX II.

MR. ROMANES'S CATECHISM.

(Reprinted from the "Journal of Education" for December, 1887, with Additions and Sequel.)

MR. ROMANES'S CATECHISM.

"There are only two true religions: one which worships, without any symbol, the Holy that is within us and around us; another which represents it by the most beautiful of symbols. Every other religion is idolatry."—GOETHE.

Mr. GEORGE J. ROMANES, while engaged in collecting materials for a forthcoming work on the Evolution of Man, drew up and distributed extensively the following minute and searching interrogations. It has seemed to me that my friends, and possibly others, will be interested in reading a full and candid *confessio fidei* on a subject which is generally avoided—the personal view of death.

1.—Do you regard the prospect of your own death (A) with indifference, (B) with dislike, (C) with dread, or (D) with inexpressible horror?

2.—If you entertain any fear of death at all, is the cause of it (A) prospect of bodily suffering only, (B) dread of the unknown, (C) idea of loneliness and separation from friends, or (D), in addition to all or any of these, a peculiar horror of an indescribable kind?

3.—Is the state of your belief with regard to a future life that of (A) virtual conviction that there is a future life, (B) suspended judgment inclining towards such belief, (C) suspended judgment inclining against such belief, or (D) virtual conviction that there is no such life?

4.—Is your religious belief, if any, (A) of a vivid order,

or (B) without much practical influence on your life and conduct?

5.—Is your temperament naturally of (A) a courageous, or (B) of a timid order, as regards the prospect of bodily pain or mental distress?

6.—More generally, do you regard your own disposition as (A) strong, determined, and self-reliant; (B) nervous, shrinking, and despondent; or (C) medium in this respect?

7.—Should you say that in your character the intellectual or the emotional predominates? Does your intellect incline to abstract or concrete ways of thought? Is it theoretical, practical, or both? Are your emotions of the tender or heroic order, or both? Are your tastes in any way artistic, and, if so, in what way? And with what strength?

8.—What is your age or occupation? Can you trace any change in your feelings with regard to death as having taken place during the course of your life?

9.—If ever you have been in danger of death, what were the circumstances, and what your feelings?

10.—Remarks.

> Es sagen's aller Orten
> Alle Herzen unter dem himmlischen Tage,
> Jedes in seiner Sprache;
> Warum nicht ich in der meinen?—FAUST.

As my experiences are very peculiar, and are indicated in a veiled form in my writings, I hope I may be excused if I make frequent reference to those writings, and at the same time withdraw the veil. This remark applies especially to my *Recollections of Pattison*. In seeking to explain his cynicism, I have used myself as a key, insomuch that the general reflections contained in the part between pages 25 and 69* give a rather minute autobiography. There is, however, the difference between his case and mine, that my ideal has always been stoical rather than saintly, and that, happily for me, no troubles have embittered my life like those that embittered his.

1 and 2.—When I am well, I regard the prospect of being dead with feelings bordering on indifference. But I feel a great dread of the bodily suffering of dying, and a still greater dread (as my temperament is extremely nervous) of my nerves becoming unstrung, and of my then being unmanned by the prospect of the unknown (*Pattison*, p. 78, especially footnote). The dread of "loneliness and separation from friends" affects me in regard to their death, not mine. As a child, I used to let spiders and wasps crawl about me; but I always felt a repugnance to touching any dead animal.

3.—"Il y a un ésotérisme inévitable, puisque la culture critique, scientifique, philosophique n'est à la portée que d'une minorité. La foi nouvelle devra trouver ses symboles. Pour le moment, elle fait plutôt aux âmes pieuses l'effet profane. . . . L'illusion n'est-elle pas indispensable ? n'est-ce pas le procédé providentiel de l'éducation ? "—AMIEL.

In dealing with this question, I propose to

* This corresponds to the part between pp. 143 and 187 in *Stones of Stumbling*, second edition. As many of my friends have my *Pattison* in the separate form, I shall hereafter refer to it in that form.

inquire whether the conception of a future life is not being gradually modified so as to suit the needs of a scientific age. Two centuries ago, the eminently devout author of *Religio Medici* felt a difficulty in believing in the Judgment Day as commonly understood. It must be owned that this difficulty is increased by modern astronomy; for the apostolic belief in a sudden, immediate, and supernatural Second Advent, to be followed by a reign of the saints on earth, is hard to reconcile with the scientific belief in the future extinction, by a slow, natural process, of all life on our planet. In short, at least one early Christian doctrine is virtually assailed by Tennyson, in his regretful lines :

"Many an Æon moulded earth before her highest, man, was born,
Many an Æon too may pass when earth is manless and forlorn."

This change of opinion may explain my seeming paradox when I say that I am sometimes embarrassed by the present meaning of the term "future life." What are the conditions of that life, and what sort of *Ego* is to survive? One clergyman represents heaven as consisting

"Of sexless souls, ideal choirs,
Unuttered voices, wordless strains."

Another (the author of *The Kernel and the Husk*)

after premising that the three lowest senses (smell, taste, and touch) are already banished from heaven, insists that sight and hearing must be banished too; but that withal the capacity of loving will be preserved. If we still retain our mental faculties, is there not a fear that, after a few billions of years, we shall grow tired of this very unearthly and inconceivable mode of existence? Or, again, if death annihilates the senses, will it leave the emotions unimpaired? In other words, if (as Dr. Maudsley, and even Professor Huxley, maintain) mind is a "function of brain," is it not as hard to suppose the individual mind surviving the decomposition of the brain, as to suppose, I will not say fire burning after the exhaustion of its fuel, but the eyesight continuing after the destruction of the optic nerve? In fact, is not modern scientific opinion tending towards the conclusion of Lucretius that, even as trees cannot live in the sky, nor fishes in the fields,

"Sic animi natura nequit sine corpore oriri
Sola, neque a nervis et sanguine longiter esse"?

It is perhaps needless to dwell on the difficulty of conceding a soul to Bushmen, and denying one to our semi-human ancestors, to gorillas, to jelly, fish; or on the difficulty of expecting that our posthumous selves will be better able to remember our present selves, than we are to remember our antenatal selves. I will, however, remark that the latter difficulty reaches further than at first sight appears. According to the philosophy of Lucretius,* it follows from the law of chances that the particles of matter which now compose my body may, at some inconceivably remote period, fall again into shape, and constitute another living man; but this *alter ego* will not be a revival of my present self, for he will not remember my present self. That is to say, the power of recollection, the *repetentia nostri*, is a necessary condition of personal identity.† Yet this necessary condition, this condition which alone prevented the apostle of annihilation from believing *literally* in the Resur-

* Lucretius III., 847—861.

† Clough, in his fifth Sonnet, *On the Thought of Death*, suggests that some dim hope might be drawn from a yet stranger hypothesis—the hypothesis apparently that, by the operation of natural laws through countless ages, worlds will be made and unmade, until, at last, *Alter ab integro seclorum nascitur ordo*. According to this weird supposition, there will haply be another England (an exact counterpart of the present), another Victorian Jubilee, and another Mr. Romanes perplexing our future namesakes with his Mortuary Catechism! Assuming the principles of Evolution, together with *infinite* time and the subjection of volition to law, few mathematicians would pronounce the recurrence of such a cycle to be quite incredible; but where will be the *repetentia nostri?*

rection of the Body, Tennyson, in *The Two Voices*, is prepared to throw overboard:

> "Some draught of Lethe might await
> The slipping thro' from state to state."

Indeed, if I rightly interpret the preceding stanza,

> " It may be that no life is found,
> Which only to one engine bound
> Falls off, but *cycles always round*,"

the poet has for a moment found himself on a standpoint not wholly unlike the Epicurean one.

A few examples will serve to show the sort of influence that such considerations as the above are exercising over Liberal Christians. An eminent Broad Church clergyman, writing to me about *The Service of Man*, says, " The religion of a people stands in a definite relation to its culture," and adds the remark (in which I heartily agree) that it is generally safer to let science and criticism work the needful changes in the national creed, than to attempt an iconoclastic subversion. Another Liberal divine tells me that he is little troubled by the mistakes which seem to be contained in the conversations reported in the Gospels; for he looks forward to a future revelation which will modify and complete Christianity, as Christianity has modified Judaism. Fourteen years ago, when I was writing my article on Tennyson's social philosophy, I talked the matter over with

Principal Tulloch. He called my attention to the doubts expressed by the poet as to whether Christianity is intended to be the ultimate phase of religious belief. I asked whether he was referring to the mention of "the Christ that is to be," and to the statement that "our little systems" of religion are but "broken lights," and that "they have their day and cease to be." He replied that, besides these passages, there are others that convey the same impression. My own comments on this topic have been made elsewhere.* I will now merely observe that, though I have no sympathy with the critic who satirised the "demi-semi-Christianity" of *In Memoriam*, I cannot but feel that the difference is fundamental between those who regard the value of religious dogmas as absolute and permanent, and those who regard it as merely relative and temporary. In fact, the difference is closely connected with the gradual transition (noticed by Pattison in his *Assize Sermon*) from the subordination of morality to religion, to the subordination of religion to morality. The less orthodox view has lately been upheld with rare honesty and courage by Canon Fremantle, who goes the length of maintaining that statements about God and the soul are mostly to be understood in a "literary," not a scientific

* *Safe Studies*, pp. 204-210.

or even a "quasi-scientific" sense. To those who censure such a symbolical exegesis as uncandid, I answer that the beginning of Genesis is commonly explained in a manner which, fifty years ago, would have been thought blasphemous; and all that enlightened Conservatives desire is that the same mode of interpretation which clergyman after clergyman applies to the first two chapters of the Bible should also be applied to the last two—that a spiritual, as opposed to a materialistic, conception should be extended from the past Paradise of Adam to the future Paradise of God. Let me add that such writers as Arthur Stanley, when speaking of the beatitude of heaven, decline to make any confident assertions about it, save that it involves Rest in God and posthumous influence for good. I lately asked a very learned and not unorthodox clergyman, whether this tendency to throw posthumous personality into the background, and to regard heaven as union with God, did not seem to him a striking peculiarity of our time. "Substantially," he replied, "this has always been the creed of Christian mystics, whether Catholic or Protestant."* The assertion surprised me; but perhaps, when one reflects on it, it throws light on the state of mind

* Compare the poem called *A Sea-change* (*Safe Studies*, p. 413).

which Christian self-abnegation, carried to its furthest point, tends to produce. " The end and aim of our life," says Kingsley, "is not happiness, but goodness. If goodness comes first, then happiness may come after; but, if not, something better than happiness may come, even blessedness." The remark clearly applies to the comparative value of happiness and blessedness, or rather of enjoyment and blessedness (these two being parts or modes of *happiness*), beyond the grave. *Faciam voluntatem tuam, sicut in terra, et in caelo,* might serve as a counterpart to the most comprehensive petition in the Lord's Prayer, and ought to satisfy, and is beginning to satisfy, our spiritual needs. Hence it appears that, as culture advances, our conception of heaven slowly changes its character; the notion of enjoyment fades into the notion of blessedness. For while, on the one hand, biology obscures our belief in posthumous enjoyment, spiritual religion, on the other hand, sets little value on enjoyment and great value on blessedness. Thus it is in such ideals as the blessedness of self-devotion, and as the Present Heaven of the Fourth Gospel, that a bond of sympathy is found between religious natures otherwise the most opposed.* *Amem te*

---

* Tauler, the fourteenth century mystic, after quoting the remarkable saying of Jesus (a saying all the more remarkable *plus quam me, neque me nisi propter te,* are words which express the aspirations of the greatest of Christian mystics; they also express the aspirations of Comte, whose favourite motto they were. "Ye are dead," says St. Paul, " and your life is hid with Christ in God." In the same spirit, a Neo-Christian might apostrophize the wise and good who have passed away : " Ye are not dead, for your life is hid with Christ in God." To each of them he might apply (in a spiritual sense) the words addressed by Beatrice to Dante :—

> " Sarai meco senza fine cive
> Di quella Roma onde Cristo è Romano."

The most extreme view of the ultimate tendency of spiritual Christianity is embodied in a passage by James Hinton (a spiritual Christian if ever there was one) :—

"Surely the desire of personal immortality is not truly a noble or worthy attitude of humanity. At least, it is not the highest. Granted it was an advance in humanity to attain to it, but may it not be a greater to give it up ? Man rose to it from less, from indifference; he should give it up for more, for self-sacrifice."

Personally, in spite of logic, and as an aid to my spiritual life, I try to maintain a beatific vision

because reported by a Synoptist), "The kingdom of God is within you," asks: "If, now, the being and essence of our soul is in heaven, and God is in it, what is to blame that we have not this heaven here, and do not know God?"

which from the nature of the case is such that, if it be an illusion, I shall never be undeceived. Let me add that, in thus *walking by faith*, I am following the example of Clough, who, while admitting that " wishes vain appear," yet, on the strength of those wishes, determines to believe in a vague something, a something in which posthumous usefulness is seemingly the chief ingredient :

> " Ah yet, when all is thought and said,
> The heart still overrules the head ;
> Still what we hope we must believe,
> And what is given us, receive ;
>
> Must still believe, for still we hope
> That, in a world of larger scope,
> What here is faithfully begun
> Will be completed, not undone."

It is, I suppose, in this limited sense—the sense of being not logical overmuch nor overwise—that Goethe understands his sweeping proposition,

Wen Gott betrügt, ist wohl betrogen.

Elsewhere he says that " Only what is fruitful is true";[*] that the art of living consists in "turning the problems of life into postulates"; and that " Man must in some sort cling to the belief that the unknowable is knowable, otherwise specu-

---

[*] This and some other sayings of Goethe recall Keats's lines :—

" Beauty is truth, truth beauty,—that is all
Ye know on earth, and all ye need to know."

lation would cease;" or rather, there would be no *modus vivendi* for philosophers with the vast majority of good men and women. (*Pattison*, p. 79.)

4.—" On ne brise pas avec le passé sans y laisser le meilleur de soi. . . . Le mythe et le rite sont l'alliage à la fois déshonorant et indispensable, sans lequel le métal serait trop pur pour servir aux usages des hommes."—SCHERER.

I call myself a philosophical Anglican. Stanley's very remarkable exposition of the Apostle's Creed (in *Christian Institutions*) has hardly a sentence which I should wish to see altered. Also, I have long since been so far a Hobbist as to think that most men, and (perhaps) all women, need religious observances (*Pattison*, p. 72), and that a philosopher's creed consists, not of the extreme conclusions to which his principles might lead, but of the sentiments and symbols with which he clothes his aspirations after the ideal, and which connect him with the poetry of the past and the present modes of thought of the religious world. "Entre tous ceux qui croient à l'idéal," says Renan, "quelles que soient leurs apparentes divergences, il n'y a qu'une différence dans la manière de parler." Our notions about man's origin and destiny are merely symbolical and relative; and, in dealing with such questions, I, as an Englishman, choose Liberal Anglicanism as the most helpful and edifying of the seemingly conflicting, but really harmonious, answers that are given by the good men and women in the many mansions of our Father's house. This very spiritualised religion has no very direct or conscious influence on my life; but, of course, the fact of belonging to a Christian community has a great indirect influence.

5.—I am very sensitive to pain. In my youth I suffered much from nervous weakness due wholly to physical causes, and have always been obliged to take great care of my health.

6.—Owing to my nervous temperament, I am unreasonably pained if my friends disapprove of my opinions and conduct. But, being aware of this weakness, I struggle against it. Friends have sometimes said that I am one of the most cheerful persons they ever met. They saw me, I suspect, under favourable circumstances.

7.—My mind is abnormally analytical. It inclines to abstract ways of thought. It is strictly theoretical; but the consciousness of this one-sidedness throws me on my guard and makes me willing to take advice, and I thus become to a certain extent practical. Doctors say that I am the best patient they ever had. My temperament is not heroic, but inclined to a stoical love of justice. I am "the one in a thousand" who, according to Bagehot (*Pattison*, p. 32), takes the world too much *au sérieux;* and, indeed, the pages 32—36 in *Pattison* are strictly autobiographical. In pages 46 to 51, I have tried to show the steps by which I have come, if not to a mild form of Pyrrhonism, at least to ethical views closely allied to those of Edmond Scherer (quoted in *Pattison*, p. 49, foot-note). When unwell, I am troubled rather than amused by such ethical puzzles as those mentioned in pp. 47, 48, and by others equally grave (*Stones of Stumbling*, p. 20). In consequence of this abnormal tendency, or rather of the need of struggling against it, I am by degrees caring less and less for Juvenal, and even Lucretius, and more and more for Horace. And, if I am sometimes afraid of becoming too partial to works written more or less in a Horatian spirit —such works as Erasmus's *Laus Stultitiae*—I console myself with the thought that, although Luther was a far greater man than Erasmus, a nation with one Luther and fifty Erasmuses would be in less imminent danger of a revolution than a nation with one Erasmus and fifty Luthers.

I feel very strong sympathies, though only with comparatively few persons. I am much affected by the painful in fiction. I have vowed never again to see " Othello " acted, and I much dislike even reading it. I feel each year an increasing need of the sympathy of good women (*Pattison*, pp. 16, 17).* I do not know one tune from another, and (perhaps owing to my eyesight) care little about pictures. But I am fond of poetry, and I am especially fascinated by the music of Shelley. My ear is fastidious about the cadence of sentences in prose.

8.—Forty-nine. — Anthropology, including Gynæcology (*Pattison*, p. 22). As a writer, I am thoroughly handicapped by the causes mentioned in the preface to *Safe Studies*. I am thus constrained to concentrate my efforts on an end which seems to me too limited and self-regarding, but which Goethe extols as the sum and substance of all wisdom :—

<blockquote>Die Welt zu kennen und sie nicht verachten.</blockquote>

Pattison called me a "*philosophe errant*" (p. 68, to end of paragraph). In my Calvinistic boyhood,

---

* A traveller in Egypt tells me that, among the random inscriptions with which tourists have defaced the monuments of antiquity, only one struck him as at all witty. A Frenchman had scrawled on one of the tombs of the kings, at Thebes, " La vie est un désert"; to which was added, by a later hand, " et la femme le chameau."

though I was thoroughly in earnest, I had not much spiritual enthusiasm. Still less was I animated by the hope of what may be called the honours and rewards of other-worldliness — a patent of posthumous nobility and a pension from the funds of eternity. On the contrary, as I vainly endeavoured to love the Author of Hell, I expected to become one of its inmates ("they that love Thee not Must burn eternally"). I am less afraid of death now than I then was! (*Stones of Stumbling*, pp. 39, 40.)

9.—I never have been in serious danger. Though sometimes very unwell, I have not spent a day indoors for twenty-six years.

10.—" Le ciel n'a rien de local, et n'est autre chose que l'union avec Dieu et avec tous les êtres bons et grands."— RENAN.

It is instructive to observe that Reuss and others give to the word " materialism " a meaning the opposite of its popular one; they use the word to denote belief in a material kingdom of God. Even Stanley has employed the word in this sense. Mr. Matthew Arnold rarely, if ever, employs it in any other sense ; he even stretches the term " materialism of the Apocalypse" so as seemingly to make it cover the belief in any conceivable form of posthumous joy or sorrow. Possibly this novel use of the term may be connected with the fact that some philosophers, and even divines,* are unable to accept the popular doctrine in its literal sense ; and, I will add, they are not unable only, but unwilling. For such unwillingness two reasons may be given. In *Safe Studies* (bottom of p. 389) I have hinted at the difficulty of believing that the Universe will ever be exempt from evil. More recently, Mr. Froude (in *Oceana*) has expressed a similar fear : " If the Devil had been capable of redemption, he would have been redeemed before he had been allowed to do so much mischief." Now, if Evil is to last as long as Good, the popular doctrine becomes simply appalling. Bee-fanciers use a net-work of wire with holes just big enough to let the working bees into the hive, and just small enough to exclude the drones. It is very hard to devise a philosophical net-work which will let in even a minimum of posthumous hope, and yet keep out even a minimum of posthumous

---

* See the extremely spiritualised account of Christ's continual presence in the Church, in Stanley's *Christian Institutions*, pp. 37, 38. Stanley insists that one's best and inmost self is not the mere conscious *Ego*, and confirms his opinion by the weighty text, "The flesh profiteth nothing, the words that I speak unto you they are spirit and they are life."

fear;* and even a very small fear of "boundless worse" is enough to poison a very ample hope of "boundless better" (*Pattison,* p. 78, foot-note). Sir James Fitzjames Stephen hints that God may be a Being of limited benevolence, or at least of limited philanthropy. From this unpleasing hypothesis might it not follow that we may, here and hereafter, be made to suffer for the welfare of other beings, higher and more numerous than we are; and that this welfare may be of a kind which we can no more fathom than a guinea-pig

---

* The doubt as to whether Ahriman will be less able to hold his own in the next world than in this, is expressed by Clough in the melancholy lines:

> "Whither depart the souls of the brave that die in the battle,
> Die in the lost, lost fight, for the cause that perishes with them?
> Are they upborne from the field on the slumberous pinions of angels
> Unto a far-off home, where the weary rest from their labour
> And the deep wounds are healed, and the bitter and burning moisture
> Wiped from the generous eyes? *Or do they linger, unhappy,*
> *Pining, and haunting the grave of their by-gone hope and endeavour?*
> Whither depart the brave?—God knows; I certainly do not."

can appreciate the far-sighted beneficence that dooms him to vivisection? Or, to put a less extreme case, even the sanguine Goethe dreaded the prospect of perpetual *ennui*. After all, is not the *Nox est perpetua una dormienda* of Catullus less dispiriting than the *Pallidula, rigida, nudula* of Hadrian?

And this brings me to my second point. The spiritual conception of heaven, as neither more nor less than union with God, is not really depressing if taken in its entirety. The same may be said even of the negations of Lucretius, as he himself has well pointed out. But, practically, it is hard to think of the loss of personal consciousness without thinking also that we shall be personally conscious of the loss. Even Pattison spoke with dismay of being deprived of his library by death, as if he expected after death to feel the deprivation. An aged kinswoman of mine expressed dread of being buried in a damp family-vault; whereupon a privileged butler broke in with the remark, "Indeed, ma'am, you needn't be the least afraid; I was down there myself the other day, and it's quite dry and comfortable." The old servant was right. If his mistress was afraid of posthumous rheumatism, it was wise to tell her that her resting-place would be dry. The same principle holds in regard to more serious consolations * Unconscious or impersonal blessedness, if presented to the imagination without being foreshortened, is seen wholly out of perspective; it seems like consciousness of unconsciousness, or rather of impotence—a sort of perpetual nightmare. And thus, if it is impossible to help trying to conceive the inconceivable, the least misleading course may be to think and speak in metaphor, so that our heaven may be defined *a state of blessedness symbolised as a place of enjoyment.*

* See Matthew Arnold's Sonnet on *The East End*, which concludes with the line:—

"Thou mak'st the heaven thou hop'st indeed thy home."

Perhaps it is in a sense not wholly unlike this that Renan makes the broad, if not cynical, assertion: "La religion n'est pas seulement philosophie, elle est art ; il ne faut donc pas lui demander d'être trop raisonnable." Does he mean that religion is no more than a politic gilding of morality and a poetic gilding of the tomb? I am tempted to add the name of another very able writer who seems to value the hope of a future life chiefly as giving a higher pulsation to the present life. It would be an exaggeration, but a pardonable one, to extract from *Marius the Epicurean* the moral, "Let us dream of immortality, for to-morrow we die."

NEOCHRISTIANITY AND NEOCATHOLICISM:
A SEQUEL.

"Ungefähr sagt das der Pfarrer auch,
Nur mit ein bischen andern Worten."
Faust.

AFTER I had replied to Mr. Romanes's Catechism, my attention was called to Mr. Mivart's most interesting and surprising article on *The Catholic Church and Biblical Criticism*,* an article which may serve to explain the Neochristian tone of my answers. To my amazement, I find that portions of those answers, and the chief arguments in my *Divine Economy of Truth*, are in accordance with the latest phase of Catholic orthodoxy. Mr. Mivart courageously exhorts his fellow-Catholics to lay aside all dogmatic bias in dealing with the results of Biblical criticism. He does not, indeed, commit himself to all the conclusions of such writers as Colenso and Kuenen; but he quotes those conclusions with sympathy, and thinks that "there can be little doubt that, in the main,

* *Nineteenth Century*, July, 1887.

they represent the truth." Among the opinions that he thus quotes are the following:—" The account, as we read it, of the deliverance from the Egyptian captivity is unhistorical, although it is not doubted that Moses existed and did lead the Israelites from Egypt. But it is not deemed probable that a line of the Bible was written by him," (what then, I would ask, becomes of the popular view of the Decalogue?) "and the whole Levitical legislation is regarded as an invention which dates from the Babylonian Captivity and times more recent." The year of Jubilee "was utterly unpractical, and was never practised." The first chapter of Genesis was written after the Captivity. The story of Jacob wrestling with God is "gross mythology" (is not, I ask, the belief in eternal punishment yet grosser?). "When I was a boy, at Oscott, I was taught that the book of Jonah was only a parable." "It is thought to be in the highest degree unlikely that Abraham, Isaac, or Jacob ever really existed, and no passage of the history of any one of them is of the slightest historical value in the old sense; though, of course, every old writing has historical value in some sense. Similarly, Daniel, dating, as it has long been concluded to do, only from about B.C. 164, is, of course, thought quite untrustworthy, and little more than a mass of fiction." " Who, in the sixteenth century, would have deemed it possible for the Church to allow that her doctrines concerning the Biblical narrative of the creation of Adam, and the miraculous formation of Eve from his rib, could accord with a belief that the ribs of both Adam and Eve were formed by natural generation in the womb of some non-human animal? Yet we have lived to witness this event." "If any Scripture narrative is detailed and distinct, it is that of the Deluge, which is also referred to in the New Testament. Nevertheless, no one now, of any account, even professes to believe the truth of the narrative we read, although it may be based on a tradition of some considerable local inundation." The author adds, in a foot-note:—"I well recollect dining at a priest's house (in or about 1870), when one of the party, the late accomplished Mr. Richard Simpson, of Clapham (a most pious Catholic and weekly communicant), expressed some ordinary scientific views on the subject of the Deluge. A startled auditor asked anxiously,—'But is not, then, the account in the Bible of the deluge true?' To which Mr. Simpson replied,—'True! of course it is true. There was a local inundation, and some of the sacerdotal caste saved themselves in a punt, with their cocks and hens.'"

I forbear to inquire in what relation Mr. Mivart

stands towards Biblical criticism as applied to the New Testament. It is enough, for my present purpose, to observe that Christ always assumed the Scriptural narratives to be in the literal sense accurate. In proof of my assertion, I will remind my readers of the reference in the Gospels to the gift which Moses commanded, and to the abomination of desolation spoken of by Daniel the prophet. To the same effect are such texts as the following:—" As it was in the days of Noe, so shall it be also in the days of the Son of Man." "Remember Lot's wife." " Your father Abraham rejoiced to see my day." " Had ye believed Moses, ye would have believed me; for he wrote of me." "If they hear not Moses and the prophets, neither will they be persuaded though one rose from the dead." It is manifest that the general view expressed in these and other passages is utterly opposed to the conclusions of Biblical critics, which are slowly leavening the educated world, and which Canon Fremantle and Mr. Mivart have quoted with substantial approval. The fact is, that enlightened Christians, whether Catholic or Protestant, are beginning to learn that their religion must adjust itself to the new conditions, and must rest rather on the spirit than on the letter of their Master's teaching. In short, we must needs admit that errors are to be found in the words, even in the plainest words, of Christ, as reported by the Evangelists.* This admission impairs, to say the least, the importance of the obscure text — "Thou art Peter, and upon this rock I will build my Church." On what foundation, then, does the Papacy rest? Whatever answer Mr. Mivart might give to this question, it seems to follow from his principles that the Catholic Church is a tree which must be judged by its fruits—that she must stand or fall with her internal evidence, must be assailed and defended on Utilitarian grounds. And I am bound to add that, on those grounds, her case is, in many respects, a strong one, stronger than that of most Protestant sects, both because of her authority and universality, and also because she is less directly and obviously committed than they are to the belief in Scriptural infallibility.† Mr.

---

* See *Stones of Stumbling*, pp. 90–103. As an eminent living ecclesiastic has expressed it, the story of Jonah rests on the authority of the Incarnate God. Let me remind my readers that I am not calling in question the doctrine of the Incarnation. Orthodox divines, such as Jeremy Taylor and Frederick Robertson (*Stones of Stumbling*, p. 114), admitted that Christ, as a Man, might have been deceived.

† Is Scherer right in maintaining that mythology and ritual are needful supports of religion? If so, criticism, by weakening the first of these props, forces religion to lean heavily on the second. This may explain why Catholicism and Ritualism are suddenly renewing their strength.

Mivart insists that she will retain her jurisdiction over faith and morals. But, in regard to the latter, he is careful to point out that Popes and councils wrongly condemned usury; and even in regard to the former he admits that the Councils of Trent and of the Vatican took an exaggerated view of Biblical inspiration.

"Little by little," he says, "the invincible advance of historical, as of other, Science permeates and transforms the whole Catholic body, and ultimately reacts upon its supreme head. While the general sentiment of Catholics remains unchanged, the Holy See remains, as a rule, sympathetically unaltering in its action. But it follows with attention, though slowly and warily, the course of scientific thought and investigation. It cannot be expected to anticipate, by positive pronouncements, what is greatly in advance of general Catholic opinion. I have what seems to me sufficient evidence that broad views are not in disfavour at the Vatican, though sudden or abrupt action is neither to be expected nor desired. It is amply sufficient if a gradual change in the knowledge, the ideas, and the convictions of the Catholic body in due time overcomes a natural reluctance to forsake a beaten path, and, by degrees, induces conformity to a new environment. The slow, silent, indirect action of public opinion does in time infallibly produce its effect; and if, now and again, authority has yielded unduly to retrograde and obstructive influences, yet, as experience has shown us with respect to Copernicanism, it may end by thoroughly adopting what was at first resisted and denounced. No doubt it may astonish and vex some persons to be told that he who is officially the leader allows himself to be led. But he does so by a wise prescience, which is the ordinary characteristic of the supreme Pontiff."

Eleven years ago, in Italy, a devout Catholic

said to me, of Pius IX.,—"In private, he is a gossiping old woman; but, for all that, as a Pope, he is infallible." Catholics seem now prepared to admit that the intellectual and moral infirmities of the Pope may affect even his public decrees, at least in regard to all matters that admit of verification. Moreover, even the province in which he is held to be infallible—the province of matters unverifiable, and yet knowable—will seem to his educated followers to be continually lessening, insomuch that they will be more and more troubled by the question,—*If he tells us of earthly things and we believe not, how can we believe when he tells us of heavenly things?* * To speak more precisely, does not the entire phenomenal world fall within the domain of the verifiable? And, as to things that lie above and beyond that world, how can we hope to conceive them with human faculties, or to express them, save metaphorically and relatively, by means of the earth-born analogies of human language—*immortalia mortali sermone notare?* Is there, then, a single religious question on which the

---

* I wonder whether, during the long misgovernment of the Papal States, pious Catholics were ever embarrassed by the text—"If a man know not how to rule his own house, how shall he take care of the Church of God?"

Holy See is the unerring exponent of absolute truth? Be this as it may, the passage above quoted from Mr. Mivart amounts to an admission that the Pope is becoming, in his relation to the Church, less and less like the rudder of a ship, and more and more like the tail of a kite; or (to use an apter illustration), less of an Absolute and more of a Constitutional Sovereign. What, then, are likely to be his lasting prerogatives? As an outsider, I, of course, speculate on the subject with extreme diffidence. But I venture to suggest that (on the hypothesis) he will retain complete control over ceremonies and discipline; he will also pronounce, on matters of faith, decisions which the Catholic masses will accept as permanently and literally accurate; while Catholic philosophers will consider them, if not as mere symbols and *broken lights*, at least as liable to revision by his successors.

A very distinguished Catholic, writing to me last year, mildly intimated a hope that his Church would hereafter modify its views on eternal punishment; but added that, at present, he could "see no footstep in that direction." This whispered protest is full of promise. One is tempted to infer from it that the time may come when (to put the matter somewhat brutally) an ordinary Catholic will say,—" The Pope bids me accept this or that doctrine, so I accept it"; whereas an intellectual Catholic will say (or think),—" As I value religious unity, I will not curse what the Pope hath not cursed; but I know he is wrong, and future Popes will agree with me." Such an application of Amiel's *ésoterisme inévitable* * is open to grave and very obvious objections. But, at any rate, let us hope that Catholics are beginning to look upon religious truth as relative, and religious knowledge as progressive. This, after all, is the fundamental point, and is especially desired by those who fear that religious evolution may be going on too fast, and who believe that a *cultus* is needful to almost every one; and that, in the process (so to say) of *Ecclesiastical Selection*, an advantage will be enjoyed by the Church which is surrounded by the brightest halo of antiquity, and which can unite the greatest number of educated and uneducated minds by a common symbol. The enlightened defenders of the faith, who think and feel thus, cannot but hope that the Catholic

---

* See the mottoes prefixed to my answers 3 and 4, in preceding article. A lady of orthodox tendencies, who was fresh from the perusal of *Literature and Dogma*, suddenly exclaimed, when reading p. 49 of Mr. Mivart's article,— " Why, this is Matthew Arnold over again!"

Church will now show that wisdom which has distinguished her in the chief crises of her long career. She took a great step when she consented to apply the principle of *E pur si muove* to our planet. She will take a greater step if she applies it to her own religious teaching. By thus taking part in the onward movement, she will give reality to an assertion which has little in common with sundry well-known utterances of Pius IX., but which is quoted approvingly by Mr. Mivart—the tolerant and wisely catholic assertion that "this is a time of drawing together of all religions and philosophies, and of the rapid growth of a universal religious consciousness with the development of human introspection. We see, on all sides of us, that ceaseless, invisible magic of thought—thought profoundly scientific, and no less profoundly spiritual—which is casting its net over all religions." In this grouping together of "all religions," is it not implied that the difference between the great and good religions of the world, however prodigious in degree, is a difference in degree rather than in kind?

TRANSLATIONS OF GREEK, LATIN, GERMAN, AND ITALIAN SENTENCES.

PREFACE TO FIRST EDITION.

Page

v. Τελείων —
> But solid food is for full-grown men.

calidâ juventâ,
> in my hot youth.

TEXT.

1. κρεῖσσον —
> Better to die outright
> Than to be miserable all one's days.

6. *Nequicquam* —
> Wise Providence in vain
> Has interposed the estranging main,
> If impious ships presume to leap
> Across the barriers of the deep.

19. *invalidi* —
> the happiness of the invalid is the concern of the invalid.

30. *bestimmt* —
> ordained in God's counsels.

32. *O! genus* —
> Unhappy race of mortals to assign
> Such crimes, such rage, to attributes divine!
> Self-torturers, what agonies your creed
> For us and for our progeny did breed!

33. *Ut puto,* —
    I think I am being made a god.
34. *fortem animum,* —
    a brave heart that knows not fear of death.
39. *ille crucem* —
    one gets a cross for guerdon, *one* a crown.
41. *Beati* —
    The blessed in the kingdom of heaven will behold the punishment of the damned to add a zest to their bliss.
43. *argumentum igneum,*
    appeal to fire by way of argument.
49. *strepitus* —
    roar of whelming Acheron.
50. *Carpe diem,*
    Enjoy to-day.

    Memento mori,
    Think of death.
52. *Si foret* —
    Democritus, restored to earth, would laugh.
54. *Beati* —
    Blessed are the dead that die in the Lord.
64. λάμπασιν —
    constantly burned by torches, they are vexed with everlasting punishments.
66. Ὦ μή 'στι —
    Words will not fright the man who fears not deeds.
67. *toto caelo* —
    by the whole extent of heaven and of hell.
69. *mox illos* —
    their destined fate awaits them ere long at the hand of a greater foe.

72. *Ingentem —*
>They weld a mighty shield to quench all the darts of the Latins.

73. *a Judæis, —*
>by Jews, for Jews, among Jews.

non nisi —
>is only conquered by obeying her.

74. *Imperium —*
>I have given a limitless empire.

75. ἐκ τοῦ στόματός σου —
>out of thy own mouth I will judge thee.

76. *immortalia —*
>we convey immortal truths in the language of mortals.

79. *Deus fallit —*
>God deceives through another.

Οὐδὲν οἴομαι —
>I think it makes no difference whether we speak of Jupiter (*i.e.*, God) as the Highest, or of Zeus, or Adonaius, or Sabaoth.

80. *Deus fallit —*
>God deceives directly.

ἐνταῦθα —
>at this place there is a hole in the sky.

Hic est —
>This is Jerusalem: I have set her in the centre of the nations, and I have set the countries round about her.

81. ὅσσα —
>All that with mortal men is reckoned a shame and dishonour,
>Theft and adulterous lust and lies and deceit of one's neighbour.

83. ἀπάτης —
   God is not averse to just deceit.
84. ὅσια πανουργεῖν,
   to commit a righteous crime.
85. *splendide mendax,*
   grand in her falsehood.
86. *quod non* —
   What fails to prove the less proves the greater.
88. *Numquid* —
   Was Paul crucified for you? Or were ye baptised in the name of Paul?
89. αἰώνιον —
   "eternal" for "brief" or "none at all."
90. Ὁμοίως —
   Equally blasphemous are those who hold that gods are born with those that say they can die.
91. *cadit quæstio,*
   there is an end of the question.
95. *esto Christus* —
   though Christ did not grow in habitual, yet he did grow in actual and practical, grace and wisdom.
97. *nanum* —
   he called Atlas a dwarf, the Æthiopian a swan.
   supra grammaticam,
   superior to grammar.
102. *Deo* —
   To please God by a lie.
104. πρῶτον ψεῦδος,
   the original falsehood.
105. κακάγγελτος ἄχη,
   the bad tidings of woe.
106. *Malunt* —
   They had rather err with Christ than be right with us.

106. *Amicus* —
  We love Christ, but we love truth more.

108. κρεῖττον —
  it is better to choose a falsehood than a real evil.

110. ἀμέραι —
  But future time is a wiser witness. For a mortal it is fitting to speak fair things concerning the deities, for the risk is less.

  ἐνέπνευσαν —
  They breathed into me a divine voice that I might unfold both the future and the past.

111. Δοκέων —
  Thinking that the messengers sent to consult the oracle were not telling the truth.

113. *Incredibile est,* —
  It is incredible that God would have spoken to the people in words that would deceive them.

  Incredibilius est, —
  It is more incredible that God will employ punishments against the people by which they will be tortured.

115. *Quid enim* —
  For what ideas can be more remote, or wider apart, or more contradictory than what is mortal and what is immortal and eternal?

125. *Haud ignota loquor,*
  I speak what I know.

127. οἰκονομίας —
  the economy of salvation.

128. *experimenta fidei,*
  trials of faith.

131. δῖνος —
  Hurly-burly is king and has expelled Zeus.

131. *Usque adeo*—
    So tyrannously is poor mortality down-trodden by an unseen power.
132. *Salve,* —
    Hail, land of Saturn, mighty mother thou
    Of fruits and mighty heroes!
135. *Vir sum,* —
    I am a man, and count nothing *feminine* foreign to me.
137. *Scurrantis* —
    "An appearance of toadyism" and "Clownish and incultured bluntness."
138. *Ens rationale,*
    "A rational being," the definition not of "*man*" (*Mensch*), but of "*the man*" (*Mann*).
    Video —
    I see the worse and commend it, but I follow the better. (An inversion of Ovid's "I see the better and follow the worse.")
139. *cum pleno salino,*
    with a full salt-cellar.
    laudando præcipere,
    to admonish while praising.
141. Οὐκ ἀγαθὸν —
    It is not good for many to bear rule.
143. ἑκών —
    unwillingly willing.
146. φιλοσοφεῖν —
    to live the philosopher's life without effeminacy.
    (Pericles' description of the Athenian character.)
148. *Stantes* —
    Our feet were in thy courts, O Jerusalem!
151. *poco di matto,*
    a little of the fool.

154. *pecca fortiter,*
   sin boldly.

   μάθε παίζειν,
   learn to be frivolous.

   amara lento —
   and with a careless laugh
   The bitter potion quaff,
   Since none, not e'en the happiest,
   Is absolutely blest.

158. Ὦ παῖδες —
   Sons of Greece, arise!
   Arise and liberate your fatherland,
   Your sons, your wives, the temples of your Gods!

159. ὁ φιλέλλην —
   The Philhellenic famous Gladstone.

   Περικλέης —
   Olympian Pericles
   Thundered and lightened and confounded Greece.

160. *cunctando —*
   by delaying restored the State.

165. ἀπορίαι,
   knotty questions.

169. *Omnia exeunt —*
   All things end in absurdity.   All is vanity.

   Imperat —
   Conscientiousness is in all cases either the master or the servant.

170. ἀκρασία —
   "incontinence" and "licentiousness."

176. βίος πρακτικός —
   the practical life . . . the theoretical life.

177. μεγαλοπρέπεια,
>   magnificence.

Εἰ ἐν τῷ ἀδίκῳ —
>   If ye were not faithful in the unrighteous mammon,
>   who will commit to your trust the true riches?

178. ἑαυτὸν τιμωρούμενος —
>   a self-tormenter . . . a self-accuser.

180. Σκέψαι —
>   Consider, boy, what sober-living means,
>   How many pleasures you will miss thereby —
>   Wine, women, dalliance, dicing, luxuries —
>   Is life worth living if you lack all these?

183. *Nil expedit*,
>   Nothing matters.

185. *Juturnam* —
>   That Juturna should rescue her poor brother.

ἄθλιον —
>   a shadow of myself,
>   Not he in sooth who once was Œdipus.

189. *Nullum tempus* —
>   God is independent of time and opportunity.

191. *Entia* —
>   Existences are not to be unnecessarily multiplied.

192. Θεοὶ —
>   Whether there are or are not gods is doubtful.

Wer darf —
>   Who dares Him name?
>   Who dares proclaim:
>   Him I believe?
>   Who that can feel
>   His heart dare steel
>   To say: I disbelieve?

195. *Was wär' ein Gott,* —
   What were a God, self-centred, free from change,
   Who watched the universe around him range?
   Nay, interfused He permeates the whole.
   Nature the body, God is nature's soul.
   Thus all that in Him lives and moves and is
   No instant can His quickening spirit miss.

196. *advertunt* —
   they turn their minds to religion,
   Since there is fear of eternal punishment in death.

197. *Aut caelum aut nihil,*
   Either heaven or nothing.

   διάνοια,
   intelligence.

198. *Unum* —
   One thing is needful. I have chosen the better part, which shall not be taken from me.

202. *vox pregnans,* —
   a pregnant utterance, big with consequences, from whose womb will issue a second progeny, portentous, perilous, damnable.

203. *spargens flores* —
   scattering flowers and paying a vain tribute of respect.

208. *Es sagen's* —
   So say
   All hearts in every clime beneath the sky;
   Each in his several way;
   And why not I in mine?

211. *Sic animi* —
   Thus mind cannot exist without a body,
   An entity divorced from nerves and blood.

212. *alter ego,*
   second self.

212. *repetentia nostri,*
>   the re-collecting of ourselves.

Alter ab integro —
>   "The world's great age begins anew."—*Shelley.*

216. *Faciam —*
>   I will do thy will in heaven as on earth.

Amem —
>   May I love thee more than myself, and myself only for thy sake.

217. *Sarai —*
>   Thou shalt be with me for ever a citizen of that Rome of which Christ is a Roman.

218. *Wen Gott —*
>   Whom God deceives is well deceived.

222. *Die Welt —*
>   To know the world and not despise it.

226. *Nox est —*
>   We must sleep through one never-ending night.

Pallidula, —
>   Poor pallid, shivering, naked soul.

228. *Ungefähr —*
>   His Reverence says almost the same,
>   Only he uses slightly different words.

234. *immortalia —*
>   to describe immortal things in mortal language.

237. *E pur si muove,*
>   And yet it moves.

www.ingramcontent.com/pod-product-compliance
Lightning Source LLC
Chambersburg PA
CBHW032136230426
43672CB00011B/2359